This book is due for return on or before the last date shown below.

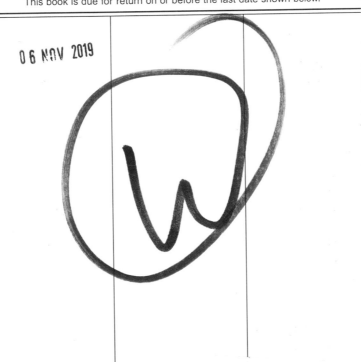

Essentia

The S

Europe 19

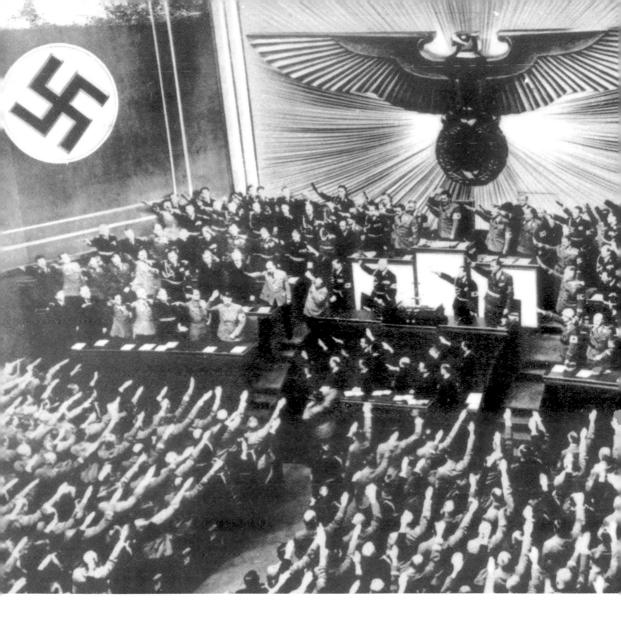

Essential Histories

The Second World War (2)

Europe 1939–1943

Robin Havers

OSPREY
PUBLISHING

First published in Great Britain in 2002 by Osprey Publishing,
Elms Court, Chapel Way, Botley, Oxford OX2 9LP, UK
Email: info@ospreypublishing.com

ISBN 1 84176 447 7

Editor: Rebecca Cullen
Design: Ken Vail Graphic Design, Cambridge, UK
Cartography by The Map Studio
Index by Bob Munro
Picture research by Image Select International
Origination by Grasmere Digital Imaging, Leeds, UK
Printed and bound in China by L. Rex Printing Company Ltd.

02 03 04 05 06   10 9 8 7 6 5 4 3 2 1

For a complete list of titles available from Osprey Publishing
please contact:

Osprey Direct UK, PO Box 140,
Wellingborough, Northants, NN8 2FA, UK.
Email: info@ospreydirect.co.uk

Osprey Direct USA, c/o MBI Publishing,
PO Box 1, 729 Prospect Ave,
Osceola, WI 54020, USA.
Email: info@ospreydirectusa.com

www.ospreypublishing.com

This book is one of six titles on the Second World War in the
Osprey Essential Histories series

Contents

Introduction

At 11.00 am on 11 November 1918, the First World War came to an end. The combined forces of Great Britain, France, Italy, and the USA had defeated the armies of Germany, Austria-Hungary, and Turkey. This war cost the lives of around 7 million combatants and a further 7 million civilians, although exact totals are difficult to ascertain. During the four years between 1914 and 1918, the 'Great War,' as it was being referred to even during the fighting, redefined the parameters of the experience of war.

The First World War was the first true 'industrial' war, where the nineteenth-century advances in technology and modes of production were harnessed to an insatiable war machine – with terrifying results. The impact of new and more efficient killing methods, backed by virtually the whole social, political, and economic infrastructure of the warring nations, produced a war of destruction unparalleled in human history. The cost of victory was such that in terms of casualty figures alone there was little to choose between winner and loser. At all levels of society – politicians, generals, ordinary soldiers, and the civilian population – there was a belief and a hope that this was the 'war to end all wars' and that in this fashion the tremendous sacrifice would not have been in vain.

Of course, tragically, the Great War did not prove to be the end of war. Instead, in many ways the Great War typified the future of war and not its past. The manner in which the war was fought, with an emphasis on the full utilization of all available resources and the involvement of the whole populace, pointed the way forward and offered a glimpse of how wars might be fought in years to come.

To those who witnessed the Armistice in 1918, the possibility of another major European conflict within their lifetime must have seemed an unimaginable horror, yet that was precisely what was to happen. Despite the shock of the Great War, of the endless lists of dead and wounded published daily in newspapers across Britain, Germany, and France, despite the widespread revulsion at war itself that the Great War engendered, Europe had barely 20 years of peace to enjoy. In 1939 Europe was plunged again into a major conflagration, and this time the cost, incredibly, would be even higher than 1914–18 in lives, in property, and, significantly, in morality.

As with the First World War, the Second World War began in Europe as a result of the actions of an aggressive Germany. Where the Second World War differed markedly from its predecessor, however, was in why the war was fought. The Second World War was not fought for material aggrandizement or for power-political advantage, although these factors had a considerable bearing on the course of the war. Fundamentally, the Second World War was fought because of political ideas – ideologies.

Political extremism in post-First World War Germany brought to power Adolf Hitler, a man convinced of his own infallibility and almost divine calling to lead Germany to victory in a race war that would establish the Germans in their rightful position of preeminence in a new global order. Hitler intended to lead the German people in a war of conquest in which the inherent superiority of the German race would be demonstrated and Germany's racial and ideological competitors would be destroyed, leaving Germany at the helm of a unified Europe. This ideological dimension underpinned the reasons for the fighting and also exercised an enormous bearing on how the fighting was conducted.

Hitler at the presentation of standards parade. (AKG Berlin)

Up to August 1939, Adolf Hitler's Germany had achieved many of her initial, territorial, ambitions through a combination of threat and belligerent diplomacy. In August 1939, Hitler felt sufficiently confident to abandon diplomacy as his principal weapon and instead to use military force to overwhelm Germany's eastern neighbor, Poland. Hitler's invasion of Poland was the event that precipitated the Second World War. Britain and France were committed to Poland's independence and had pledged to come to her aid in the event of a German attack. The British and French governments issued an ultimatum to Germany, demanding her withdrawal. Hitler dismissed this threat, believing that the French and British were unlikely to do anything to stop the German invasion. When Germany failed to respond to the ultimatum, Britain and France were brought into another war and the Second World War was born.

However, unlike the attritional struggle and stalemate of the First World War, the Second World War was fought to quite a different tempo, initially at least. In the first nine months of the Second World War, Germany's military triumphs were nothing less than astonishing. She invaded and conquered Poland in little over a month, aided by an expedient alliance with the Soviet Union, which enthusiastically helped Germany to dismember and divide Poland. During the course of this opening campaign, Britain and France did nothing to come to Poland's aid.

The German invasion of Poland was followed by an attack on Norway and then, when Hitler's forces were fully prepared, on the combined British and French forces in the west. In a brilliant, if fortuitous campaign, the French and their Belgian, Dutch, and British allies (the British in the form of a large army dispatched to the Continent) were defeated in barely six weeks. By June 1940 all continental Europe, from Moscow to Madrid, had succumbed to Germany, was allied to her, or was neutral. Hitler's Germany had achieved in a little over nine months what Imperial Germany, the Germany of Kaiser Wilhelm, had failed to do over the course of four years.

After the fall of France and the loss of much of the British army's heavy equipment during the fighting and the hasty evacuation from Dunkirk, Britain faced a desperate battle to maintain her freedom against what appeared to be an irresistible tide of German success. During what became known as the 'Battle of Britain,' a struggle in effect for air superiority, Germany suffered her first major setback of the war. Tenacious Royal Air Force (RAF) fighter pilots, mainly British but with many Australians, Americans, Canadians, New Zealanders, Poles, Czechs, and others among them, denied the Germans the freedom of the skies that they needed to launch their projected invasion of the British Isles.

Unable to implement Operation Sea Lion, the code name for the invasion of Britain, Hitler instead began planning for what he considered to be the main prize: the Soviet Union. Before this, however, Hitler's forces also occupied Greece and Yugoslavia and became active in North Africa in support of Italian forces. On 22 June 1941, Hitler's armed forces turned eastwards, attacking the Soviet Union in Operation Barbarossa and widening the war dramatically. On 12 July, Britain and the Soviet Union signed a mutual assistance agreement to fight their common enemy together. On 11 December 1941, following the surprise Japanese attack on the American Pacific fleet at Pearl Harbor, Germany also declared war on the USA, widening the war still further and, in doing so, increasing the odds considerably on conclusive German victory (see *The Second World War (1) The Pacific War* and *The Second World War (5) The Eastern Front* in this series).

Adolf Hitler's Germany, at the zenith of her power, now faced a formidable array of opponents: the largest empire in the world, the British; the state with the largest armed forces, the Soviet Union; and the nation that possessed the largest economy and probably the greatest latent potential of all, the USA. The German offensive in the Soviet Union, after some impressive early success, did not bring about the decisive and swift victory that was required. Whether Germany had a chance to win this war decisively is a matter of considerable debate. Certainly, her failure to knock the Soviet Union out of the war before the USA was able to make her impact felt effectively meant that Germany could only realistically achieve a draw of some description. The ferocity with which Germany had waged the war, however, especially in the east, meant that her foes were in no mood for compromise and, following a conference at Casablanca in early 1943, demanded nothing short of unconditional surrender.

Once the initiative had passed from Germany to her opponents and the war became attritional, there could be only one logical outcome, although Germany's resistance to the bitter end meant that this conclusion was reached with the loss of more, rather than fewer, lives and with greater damage. From early 1943, after the Battle of Stalingrad, the Soviets gradually pushed back the German forces and in June 1944 the western allies invaded occupied France and began to drive the Germans back from the west. The hard-pressed Germans, obliged to fight a two-front war and bombed mercilessly from the air, fought on until May 1945. On 8 May 1945, the new German Chancellor, Admiral Dönitz – Hitler's successor of a mere eight days – surrendered unconditionally to the Allies: Great Britain, the USA, the Soviet Union, and France.

In the ruins of Hitler's Germany – the Reich he had claimed would last 1,000 years – it was, symbolically, the USA and the Soviet Union who linked up first on the Elbe River. These two extra-European powers would be the new determinants of the world order in the postwar years, as Britain and France, the two preeminent European powers, reluctantly redefined their respective roles on the world stage, exhausted by the demands of two wars in short succession.

The first four years of the Second World War – the period covered in this book – witnessed the rise and gradual fall of German hegemony in Europe. The book examines how the Second World War began, first by looking at the legacy of the First World War and then by exploring Adolf Hitler's actions, which precipitated the war itself. The book also examines the role of Nazi ideology in influencing how the war would be fought. The major campaigns of the first four years are then chronicled: the German invasion of Poland; the Norway campaign; the fall of France and the Low Countries; the 'miracle' of Dunkirk and then the subsequent 'Battle of Britain.' The book describes how the British tried to hit back at German-occupied Europe, with the disastrous Dieppe raid and the development of the controversial strategic bomber offensive. There are also accounts of life in occupied Germany and of the experiences of war for both a civilian and a soldier.

Chronology

1938 **12 March** German army marches into Austria
13 March Austria is incorporated into the greater German Reich
28 March Adolf Hitler encourages the German minority in Czechoslovakia to agitate for the break-up of the state
11 August Czechs open negotiations with the Germans after Britain and France apply pressure on them to do so
12 August Germans begin to mobilize
4 September Sudeten Germans reject offers of autonomy for the Sudetenland
7 September The French begin to mobilize
12 September Hitler demands that the Czechs concede to German claims on the Sudetenland
15 September British Prime Minister Chamberlain visits Hitler at his mountain retreat at Berchtesgaden, where Hitler affirms his determination to annex the Sudetenland completely
18 September Britain and France agree to try to persuade the Czechs to concede territory in which there are more than 50 percent Germans
22 September Chamberlain meets Hitler at Godesberg, where Hitler demands the immediate German occupation of the Sudetenland
29 September After negotiations, Chamberlain, Mussolini, Daladier, and Hitler agree to transfer the Sudetenland to Germany while guaranteeing Czechoslovakia's existing borders

30 September Hitler and Chamberlain sign the 'peace in our time' document
1 October Germans begin their occupation of the Sudetenland
5 October Czech premier, Benes, resigns

1939 **15 March** German troops occupy Prague
28 March Hitler denounces the 1934 nonaggression pact with Poland
16 April Soviet Union proposes a defensive alliance with France and Britain, but this offer is rejected
27 April Britain introduces conscription; Hitler abnegates the 1935 Anglo-German naval treaty
22 May Hitler and Mussolini sign the 'Pact of Steel'
11 August Belated Anglo-French overtures to Soviet Union
23 August Soviet Union and Germany unveil a nonaggression treaty, the Molotov–Ribbentrop Pact, which contains a secret clause concerning the dismemberment of Poland
25 August Britain and Poland sign a mutual assistance pact
28 August Poles reject negotiations with Germans
1 September Germans invade Poland
2 September Britain and France issue Germany with ultimatums over Poland
3 September Britain and France declare war on Germany
17 September Soviet Union invades eastern Poland

30 September Soviet Union and Germany partition Poland; the BEF arrives in France

1940 **9 April** Germany invades Norway
14 April British forces land in Norway
2 May British forces evacuated from Norway
10 May Chamberlain resigns; Churchill takes over as Prime Minister; Germany invades France
28 May Belgium surrenders
29 May–3 June Operation Dynamo
22 June France surrenders
June–September Battle of Britain

1941 **22 June** Operation Barbarossa begins
December Japan bombs Pearl Harbor; Germany declares war on USA

1942 **26 May** Anglo–Soviet treaty on greater cooperation in war against Germany
14 August Raid on Dieppe fails

1943 **January** Churchill and Roosevelt demand 'unconditional surrender' of Nazi Germany
February Last German forces surrender at Stalingrad
July Allied landings in Sicily.

The gathering storm

There are many considerations that made the outbreak of the Second World War possible. What made the war inevitable was one man: Adolf Hitler. Once Hitler had achieved power in Germany, war was certain to come. The combination of circumstances that allowed a man like Hitler to seize power, maintain it, and then take the opportunities presented to him on the international stage, however, were less inevitable and far more complicated.

Hitler made skillful use of the political and economic turmoil of post-First World War Germany. He also capitalized on the underlying sentiment in the army and among more right-wing elements of German society, that Germany's defeat in the First World War was attributable to a 'stab in the back' by socialists and communists at home, rather than to a conclusive military defeat, which of course is what had actually happened. Hitler was able to focus these feelings more strongly courtesy of the provisions of the Treaty of Versailles, which ended the war. This constant reminder of Germany's national humiliation was a useful tool for Hitler's broader aims.

Hitler's vehicle to power was the Nazi Party, 'Nazi' being an abbreviation of *Nationalsozialistische*. Hitler brought his personal dynamism to this rather directionless party and with it his own ideas. In particular, he brought a 'virulent strain of extreme ethnic nationalism' and the belief that war was the means by which the most racially pure and dynamic people could affirm their position as the rulers of a global empire. Mere revisions of the map were inconsequential in Hitler's larger scheme of things. His ultimate goals lay in the east, where a war of annihilation was to be waged against the Soviet Union.

The Soviet Union was the incarnation of many evils as far as Hitler was concerned. His eventual war in the east was designed to destroy the 'Judeo-Bolshevik' conspiracy that

The signing of the Treaty of Versailles, signed by the Allied and Associated Powers and Germany, on 28 June 1918. (Ann Ronan Picture Library)

he saw emanating from Moscow, and to remove the Slavic population, considered by Nazi ideology as *Untermenschen* or subhumans. The territory obtained would be effectively colonized by people of Germanic stock, enlarging and ensuring the survival of the Third Reich. It was this element that distinguished 'Hitler's war' from previous wars and Hitler's Germany from the Germany of the Kaisers. Germany, however, was no stranger to conflict.

A united Germany

The nation state of Germany is a comparatively new phenomenon. Only in 1871 did a united Germany come into existence. In 1866 the German state of Prussia decisively defeated Austria in the Seven Weeks' War and in doing so assured Prussian dominance of the collection of German-speaking states in central and eastern Europe. Following Prussia's further success against France, in the Franco-Prussian War of 1870, a united Germany was proclaimed on 18 January 1871, in the Hall of Mirrors at the Palace of Versailles, just outside Paris. Prussia was the largest German state and also the most advanced economically and militarily. The Prussian

capital, Berlin, became the capital of this new European power and the Prussian king, at this point Wilhelm I, became the first Emperor or *Kaiser* of a united Germany.

The ambitions of the new state grew considerably with the accession to the throne of Imperial Germany of Kaiser Wilhelm II in 1888. Wilhelm's foreign policy was an aggressive one. He sacked his Chancellor, Bismarck, the man whose political maneuvering had largely created the united Germany, and determined on building Germany up into a world, rather than just a European power. Wilhelm's reckless desire to acquire colonial possessions met with little success in the years prior to 1914, but his determination to build a navy to rival the British one inevitably brought him into conflict with Britain.

Wilhelm, himself a grandson of Queen Victoria, allowed and encouraged a belief that Germany must provide for herself in an increasingly competitive world. In 1914 the opportunity came for Germany to throw herself against France, her nearest continental rival. When Archduke Franz Ferdinand, the heir to the throne of Austria-Hungary, was assassinated, Germany grasped her chance enthusiastically. The rival power

Bismarck in the Hall of Mirrors, Versailles. (AKG Berlin)

blocs, complicated alliance systems, and powder keg diplomatic atmosphere ensured that there was no repetition of the comparatively short wars of the mid- to late nineteenth century. The First World War, the Great War, had begun.

Military defeat and the Weimar Republic

After four years of appalling slaughter, Germany was defeated decisively in 1918. Kaiser Wilhelm abdicated just days before the Armistice was signed and a left-wing government took over the country. This new government was obliged to sign what the Germans, at least, perceived to be an unfair diktat masquerading as a peace settlement. The Treaty of Versailles that formally brought the war to an end was a controversial settlement. The treaty laid the blame for starting the war squarely upon German, saddled her with enormous reparations payments, and also took away large areas of Germany territory, in many cases creating new states.

All of these considerations would have a bearing on the outbreak of the Second World War, although in all probability the failure to implement the treaty adequately was as serious a factor as its provisions. Of particular significance also was the fact that the government that signed the humiliating treaty found itself being blamed for doing so, when in reality it had little choice. The Social Democrats were also blamed for the German capitulation – many right-wingers and particularly the army considered that the German people had not been defeated, but rather had been 'stabbed in the back' by the government. This myth gained widespread credence in Germany during the interwar years.

In the early years after the war, Germany suffered along with most of the continent and political extremism was rife. The new German republic was established in the small town of Weimar, later to become famous for its proximity to the Buchenwald concentration camp. Hence this period of German history, the first ever of genuine German democracy, is known as the Weimar Republic. Weimar was chosen in preference to Berlin as the site of the new government because of Berlin's associations with Prussian militarism. Berlin was also a less than safe place.

The Weimar government was assailed from both sides of the political spectrum. Extremists fought in many large German cities and occasional attempts were made by left and right to overthrow the government; the insurrection led by Wolfgang Kapp (known as the 'Kapp Putsch') was one of the most serious. The constitutional system that underpinned the Weimar government also complicated matters. The system was so representative of political opinion that it produced only minority governments or fragile coalitions that had little opportunity to achieve anything. Meanwhile, international tensions rose when Germany suspended her reparations payments, as a result of which the French, eager to draw every pfennig from the Germans, occupied the Ruhr region in 1923. These international concerns were exacerbated by soaring inflation, with the German mark being traded at 10,000 million to the pound.

Hitler's rise to power

Amidst all this social, economic, and political turbulence, one radical among many was making a name for himself. Adolf Hitler, an Austrian by birth, had served in the German army throughout the First World War. In 1923 Hitler, who had become leader of the fledgling Nazi Party (then the German Workers' Party, *Deutsche Arbeiter Partei*) by virtue of his personal dynamism and skills of oratory, organized his first clumsy attempt to seize power. However, the Munich Putsch, on 9 November 1923, was a failure and earned him five years in Landsberg prison.

Despite the sentence, Hitler served only nine months in rather plush conditions. The authorities, many of whom had some

The freikorps (above) were dissolved in 1921 and many members later went on to join Hitler's SA.

sympathy for Hitler's position, were persuaded to release him early, after Hitler temporarily resigned the leadership of the Nazi Party and agreed to refrain from addressing public meetings on political issues. However, Hitler neatly circumvented these restrictions by moving his meetings into the private homes of his wealthier supporters.

While Hitler was in jail, dictating his memoirs and thoughts, later to be published as *Mein Kampf*, the situation in Germany improved considerably. A new scheme, the Dawes Plan, was accepted to reschedule Germany's repayments, which now reflected more closely Germany's ability to pay. It also allowed Germany to borrow substantially, mainly from the USA, and fueled a brief flurry of credit-induced economic prosperity. Germany later ratified a more comprehensive restructuring of the payments in the Young Plan, which improved her economic situation.

Similarly, the efforts of a new Chancellor, Gustav Stresemann, led to Germany entering the League of Nations in 1926 and signing the Treaty of Locarno with Britain and

France, which helped to thaw the international situation. This treaty confirmed the existing borders of the participating states of western Europe. The prevailing feeling of reconciliation appeared to usher in a more constructive period of international relations. Importantly, however, Locarno failed to guarantee the frontiers of Germany in the east, suggesting to many in Germany that the western powers would not be as concerned if Germany were to attempt to reclaim lost territory there.

However, the improvements in Germany's position by 1929 were undone totally by an unforeseen event that would have tremendous ramifications for the world at large. On 29 October 1929 came the Wall Street crash. The immediate effect was that all the American loans that had been artificially buoying up the world economy were recalled. The effects on the global economy were dramatic enough, but Germany, whose tenuous economic recovery had been fueled by extensive borrowing from the USA, was among the hardest hit. This new round of economic hardship gave Hitler another opportunity to make political capital, and he seized it with both hands.

Political violence on the streets of German cities characterized the years between 1929

Chaos in the streets during the Wall Street crash. (Topham Picturepoint)

and 1933 as Nazi fought communist and Germany's economy labored under the pressures of worldwide recession and reparations. It was Hitler and the Nazis who promised a brighter future for Germany, and on 29 January 1933, the President of the German Republic, Paul von Beneckendorff und Hindenburg, appointed Adolf Hitler as Chancellor of Germany. In the elections of the following March, the Nazi Party received 44 percent of all votes cast. Even in the overly representational system of the Weimar Republic, this was still sufficient to give the Nazis 288 out of the 647 seats in the Reichstag. Hitler made ample use of his position, passing various 'Enabling Laws' to make him effectively a legal dictator.

Once Hitler took power, he began immediately to destroy the old structures of society and rebuild them in the mode of National Socialism. All political parties other than the Nazi Party were banned. Progressively, Jews were excluded from

society and publicly shunned, culminating in the anti-Jewish pogrom of *Kristallnacht* in 1938 when Jewish property was vandalized. Concentration camps were also opened for 'undesirables' where hard work was the order of the day – the extermination role of these camps was as yet in the future. Hitler attempted to get Germans back to work with an ambitious program of public works, the planning and construction of the *Autobahnen* being the most famous.

Hitler was not above removing anyone who stood in his way. On 'the night of the long knives' he ordered the deaths of his old comrade and supporter Ernest Röhm, head of the Sturmabteilung (SA), and several hundred senior SA men. The SA was a large group of paramilitaries who had provided some of Hitler's earlier supporters. These men were a private army for the Nazi Party

Germany and Central Europe after the Treaty of Versailles

ESTONIA

LATVIA

LITHUANIA

DENMARK

NORTH SEA

SCHLESWIG-HOLSTEIN

EAST PRUSSIA

Polish corridor

GREAT BRITAIN

London

HOLLAND

Elbe

Berlin

POLAND

BELGIUM

Rhine

GERMANY

1

RHINELAND

2

Paris LUXEMBOURG SAARLAND

3

CZECHOSLOVAKIA

4

FRANCE

Rhône

SWITZERLAND

AUSTRIA HUNGARY

1. Rhineland demilitarized.
2. Saarland under League of Nations administration until 1935.
3. Alsace-Lorraine returned to France.
4. Upper Silesia ceded to Poland after plebiscite.

YUGOSLAVIA

ITALY

M E D I T E R R A N E A N S E A

N

☐ Germany in 1918

Land lost by Germany as a result of the Treaty of Versailles in 1919

0   200 miles

0   250 km

and kept order at political meetings as well as engaging in physical battles with communists and other opponents. Increasingly, however, Hitler doubted the loyalty of Röhm, and the activities of the SA alienated the army, whose support Hitler needed. In the wake of the SA emerged the Schutzstaffel (SS), under Heinrich Himmler. In removing the army's potential rivals, the SA, Hitler hoped to get the army more firmly on his side. Hitler also made the army swear a personal oath of allegiance to him as the 'Führer of the German Reich and people and Commander-in-Chief of the armed forces.'

At this time, Hitler began to revise the Treaty of Versailles. The treaty affected Germany in a number of ways. First, she lost in the region of one-eighth of her territory and one-tenth of her population: the provinces of Alsace and Lorraine, seized by Prussia as spoils of the 1870 war, were returned to France; Eupen-Malmedy was given to Belgium, and Schleswig-Holstein to Denmark. The most serious territorial losses were in the east, where Germany lost a large area of West Prussia to the recreated state of Poland. This left East Prussia cut off from Germany and accessible, by land, only across Polish territory – known as the 'Polish Corridor.' The city at the head of this corridor, Danzig, was to be a free city under the auspices of the League of Nations. Germany also lost territory to the new state of Czechoslovakia, created out of the ruins of the Austro-Hungarian Empire.

Importantly, these territorial losses in the east did not include a transfer of their German-speaking populations, who largely remained in situ and ripe for use as political pawns in the future. At the end of the Second World War, when Germany was once again dismembered, the Allies did not make the same mistake again and expelled millions of Germans to ensure that they would not become troublesome and vocal minorities in the future. Under the Treaty of Versailles, Germany was also forbidden to unite with Austria, the Rhineland was to be demilitarized in perpetuity, and all Germany's colonies were handed over to the Allies.

Germany's military capabilities were drastically reduced; she was to have no major navy or air force and only 100,000 men in the army. Germany was also required to pay a huge indemnity, £6,600 million. Perhaps the most controversial provision of the treaty was Article 231, the so-called war guilt clause, in which Imperial Germany, and Germany alone, was blamed for starting the war.

Much has been written about how the Treaty of Versailles played a role in the outbreak of the Second World War. Despite what turned out to be Marshal Foch's accurate prediction, that 'this [the treaty] is not a peace but an armistice for 20 years,' the treaty itself did not *cause* the Second World War. It certainly failed to prevent another war, but then the treaty was never enforced as it was originally meant to be. Nevertheless, the Treaty of Versailles provided Adolf Hitler with a useful vehicle for inciting German hatred. The inequities represented by the treaty, in particular the losses of land that in many cases had been German for hundreds of years, were a daily reminder that Germany had lost the war. Although the provisions of the treaty itself did not lead directly to war, the fact of the treaty was enormously useful for Hitler's purposes.

Hitler did not take long before he began to repudiate various elements of the treaty. In March 1935 he reintroduced conscription into Germany, announced that the peacetime army would be raised to 500,000 men, and also brazenly announced the existence of an army air arm, the Luftwaffe. All were in direct contravention of the treaty, yet none drew firm responses from the Allies, Britain and France. Hitler also signed a naval agreement with Britain allowing the new German navy a proportion of the tonnage of the Royal Navy.

In 1936 Hitler chanced his arm still further by reoccupying the demilitarized Rhineland. France was concerned by this resurgence of German confidence, but was unwilling to act without firm support from Britain. Many historians have interpreted this failure to act against Hitler at this early stage as disastrous. Certainly Hitler gained

German troops reenter the Rhineland on 7 March 1936.
(AKG Berlin)

strength from his inital successes, becoming
convinced that the British and French were
too weak to stop him. Indeed, during the
reoccupation of the Rhineland, German
troops were instructed to retreat if the
French merely looked as though they would
offer some resistance. On 14 October 1933,
Germany withdrew from the League of
Nations. In 1936 she sent men, aircraft, and
naval vessels to fight in the Spanish Civil
War, providing the new armed forces with a
real proving ground for their tactics and
equipment.

Responses to Hitler

There are several reasons why little was done
to stop Hitler at this early juncture. First,
although Hitler was considered something
of an extremist, he was not yet the
megalomaniac the world now knows him to
be. Although much of what was to follow
was mentioned in *Mein Kampf*, few outside
Germany had bothered to read this long and
dull work. Paradoxically, Hitler was also
considered a positive development by many.
His dynamic leadership appeared to bring
badly needed order and stability to
Germany. David Lloyd-George, the wartime
British Prime Minister, spoke of Hitler's

achievements in getting the unemployed back to work and famously visited Hitler in Germany, being greeted by him as 'the man who won the war.' Lloyd-George was neither the first nor the last senior politician to be hoodwinked by Hitler.

The new Germany was also considered to be a valuable bulwark against the threat of communism from the east and Hitler's authoritarian regime was seen as a small price to pay for such reassurance. This fear of communism was a significant force in interwar Europe and it prevented any meaningful development of an alliance between the western allies and the Soviet Union until Hitler had shown his hand completely.

Importantly, there were many on the Allied side who believed the Treaty of Versailles to be a mistake, neither harsh enough to punish nor lenient enough to conciliate. The treaty was greeted with less enthusiasm than might have been expected in some quarters. The eminent British economist John Maynard Keynes resigned from his position with the British team responsible for negotiating the treaty amid disagreements over what form it would eventually take. Keynes's criticism found form in his book *The Economic Consequences of the Peace*, and this began the subtle changing of opinion, at the highest levels at least, in Britain. Such feelings help explain why there was widespread antipathy toward enforcing such a treaty.

There were other factors that militated against a more unitary front towards the growing threat of Nazi aggression in Europe. There was still memory of the horrendous legacy of the First World War. The generation of politicians in office in the 1930s had served in the trenches and knew firsthand the cost of such a war. These sentiments had a profound echo in the public at large with the League of Nations Peace Ballot and the famous Oxford Union debate (when undergraduates debated and

passed the motion 'this house will not fight again for King and Country') all contributing to an air of pacifism. The belief that Hitler was at worst an ambiguous figure combined with an overwhelming reluctance to fight another war led to a profound inertia and perhaps an unwillingness to recognize the threat even when it became overt.

Underscoring the political vacillation and popular mood was a concrete economic reason for avoiding a costly conflict. The Wall Street crash and the consequent Great Depression had left most industrialized economies significantly weaker. The financial muscle required to prosecute another war was simply unavailable through the early to mid-1930s. Ironically, even though Nazi Germany and Roosevelt's America introduced programs (such as the New Deal in the USA) to stimulate the economy, it was rearmament that finally got men back to work.

Portrait of J. M. Keynes, the famous British economist. (Topham Picturepoint)

The road to war

The Second World War was fought between Britain, France, the USA, Poland, the Soviet Union and assorted smaller countries on one side, and Germany, Italy, Romania, and Hungary on the other. Matters are slightly complicated by the fact that the Soviet Union was allied to Germany from August 1939 until June 1941 when Germany attacked her. We will look here at Germany, France, Britain, and Poland, and make smaller mention of the other participants.

Germany

The German armed forces at the outbreak of the war were perhaps the best prepared for the ensuing conflict, although Germany did not possess the largest army in 1939. The Germans had worked out how best to utilize the various new technological developments in weaponry and harnessed them effectively to traditional German tactics as well as originating new tactical ideas.

In the aftermath of the First World War, the German military faced a sobering reappraisal of their position. Despite the many variations of the 'stab in the back' idea, that Germany had lost the war not because of military defeat but instead by the actions of left-wing elements at home, the German armed forces had been decisively defeated by 1918. Senior German officers were only too aware of where their shortcomings lay and set about addressing them.

The German armed forces responded to defeat with a thorough examination of the reasons that underpinned it, and set about providing practical military solutions to their problems. However, just as Germany had suffered extensive territorial loss as a result of the Treaty of Versailles, so too did she suffer considerable readjustment of the manning

and equipment levels of her armed forces. In November 1918, at the time of the Armistice, the Imperial German army could field in the region of 4 million men. After the Versailles settlement she was restricted to a formation that numbered only 100,000 troops, of whom 4,000 were officers. While this number was comparatively small, the men of the '100,000' Army would provide the nucleus of the enlarged army and their intensive training and proficiency would prove to be invaluable.

As well as these limitations on manpower, the German army was prohibited from possessing or developing tanks and the German air force was abolished altogether. The German navy, much of which had been scuttled at Scapa Flow as it was due to be handed over to the British, was confined to a few larger surface vessels from the pre-*Dreadnought* era, but was forbidden to have U-boats at all. These apparent disadvantages were overcome in a number of ways.

Under the enthusiastic and skillful leadership of Colonel-General Hans von Seeckt, many of the arrangements agreed upon at Versailles were sidestepped or negated. First, the German military spent a great deal of time *thinking* about the way in which their forces might be employed to face a larger enemy and also about why they had failed to win a victory between 1914 and 1918. While the Germans were denied access to new equipment, they considered how they might employ such equipment in the likely event of restrictions on Germany being lifted.

The Germans also went to considerable lengths to circumvent the restrictions on equipment. In 1922 a bilateral agreement was forged between Germany and Bolshevik Russia, the two pariah states of Europe, to cooperate on military matters. The Germans gained training areas away from the prying eyes of the Allies, while the Soviet Union

Hans von Seeckt (right). (AKG Berlin)

received technical aid. The training of pilots was also carried out clandestinely, with many pilots learning the principles of flight through the new glider clubs that grew during the 1920s and 1930s. When Hitler came to power in January 1933, he brought with him a resolve and an ideology to make Germany a great power once again. His accession brought a new commitment to rearmament and a determination to reassert Germany's international position.

When the new German army was unleashed on the Poles in 1939, and especially against the Anglo-French forces in 1940, it exhibited a flexible technique of command and control that proved the difference between the German soldiers and their opponents. This idea had its roots in the partially successful German spring offensive of 1918 and stressed the idea of *Aufragstaktic* or mission command. This focused on the need for all officers and NCOs to take decisions to achieve the goal of their mission, and encouraged initiative and freedom of action on the ground rather than waiting for orders from on high. This flexibility was aided by the development of wireless communications and the fact that all German tanks were equipped with radios.

In 1932 a Germany army captain named Bechtolsheim gave a lecture on German principles of war to the United States Artillery School. He stressed the following ideas:

The German Army has of course its principles as to what is to be done in war, but – please mark this well – no stereotyped rules as to how it is to be done. We believe that movement is the first element of war and only by mobile warfare can any decisive results be obtained ... to do always what the enemy does not expect and to constantly [sic] change both the means and the methods and to do the most improbable things whenever the situation permits; it means to be free of all set rules and preconceived ideas. We believe that no leader who thinks or acts by stereotyped rules can ever do anything great, because he is bound by such rules. War is not normal. It cannot therefore be won by rules which apply in peacetime.

These ideas found their most effective expression in the employment of tanks and supporting arms acting in concert, and they were aided by the ideas of General Heinz Guderian, often called the 'father of the Panzers' (tanks). The sum total of German ideas of mission command and new technology would prove devastating in the early years of the Second World War and would introduce a new word to the military lexicon, *Blitzkrieg*.

Great Britain

At the end of the First World War, it was the British army that appeared to lead the world in terms of effective war fighting. The British skill in utilizing the all-arms concept (the interaction of artillery, tanks, infantry, and air power) had been very apparent at the end of 1918. By 1939, however, this effective lead had been lost. The reasons why this state of affairs developed are several.

Britain, like most of the major combatants in the First World War, was 'war weary.' In the late 1920s a rash of books was published detailing the experiences of British troops in the war. Almost all written by officers, these books played a significant role in defining or redefining the popular British perceptions of that conflict. Works such as Siegfried Sassoon's *Memoirs of a Fox Hunting Man*, Edmund Blunden's *Undertones of War*, and Robert Graves' *Goodbye to All That* (to name but three) meshed well with a general sense that the war was a tragedy, and rather eclipsed and replaced other modes of remembrance. Certainly at this time there were few books that celebrated the war as an unambiguous victory. In tandem with this literary response there came a wider, popular revulsion against war in the more general sense, underscored by the Peace Ballot. With this mood in the country and little money generally, it is hardly surprising that defense budgets were slashed.

In tandem with widespread anti-war sentiment, Britain also found herself in a precarious economic position. Having

Siegfried Sassoon was one of the many poets and writers who took part in the First World War, and whose experiences colored their writings. (Topham Picturepoint)

entered the war as the global economy's principal creditor – the one to whom the most money was owed – she finished it as one of the largest debtor states. The cost of the war had been enormous, absorbing British reserves and also bringing about the loss of many of Britain's overseas markets when production of consumer goods was switched to war materials. At the end of the war, British producers found that many of their prewar markets had been taken over by other countries, notably the USA. Indeed, it was the USA that emerged as the economic victor after 1918. Having capitalized on the absence of traditional European competition for trade and markets between 1914 and 1918, she also lent large amounts to the other Allied participants.

British strategy in the event of another war initially focused upon facing the imagined threat of air attack. The idea that 'the bomber will always get through'

informed British defense thinking from 1934. To this end, priority was given to building up the Royal Air Force (RAF) and establishing the new 'radar' system to cover the British coast. The Royal Navy, although no longer the unchallenged master of the seas, was still a formidable force. The British army was the only fully mobile army in 1939 and the British Expeditionary Force (BEF) that was dispatched to France in 1939 was still a useful formation at 160,000 men. The interwar debate about the role of the tank in the British army had largely been resolved by 1939. The resolution had come in favor of those who believed that the tank should be the essential element of any formation, but acting alone, not as a component of a cohesive all-arms grouping.

France

In the interwar years, a great deal of security, real or imagined, was derived from the very existence of the French army. In March 1933, two months after Adolf Hitler became Chancellor of Germany, Winston Churchill made one of his customary and oft-quoted exclamations, declaring: 'thank god for the French army!' To such as Churchill, still a lone voice in the political wilderness in 1933, the French army was a significant bulwark against future German aggression. Few in Britain, however, agreed with him. Indeed there were many who saw the posturing of France with regard to Germany as the real threat to European stability and not Germany herself.

In many ways, France's experience of the First World War was quite different from that of her British allies, and it certainly exercised a far greater influence on her subsequent military organization, doctrine, and tactics. While the British army fought in several different theaters and pioneered the employment of tanks and the adoption of all-arms techniques of fighting toward the end of the war, with great success, the French successes between 1914 and 1918 were grounded in determinedly holding a defensive line. This static mentality found both its most eloquent expression and a source of national grandeur in the heroic fighting at Verdun, where the French army had endured horrific casualties yet had prevailed. Despite French offensive success and their own positive experiences of all-arms conflict toward the end of the First World War, French losses had been so significant between 1914 and 1918 that few Frenchmen would willingly go to war in the future.

The idea of the defense had a special poignancy for the French, as their losses in the First World War were taken on French soil and in defense of *La République*. It was no wonder, then, that future defensive arrangements should seek to learn from French successes and

The Maginot Line, constructed at massive cost, was the cornerstone of French defensive strategy. (Ann Ronan Picture Library)

also to build on them to such an extent that the devastation of 1914–18 would not be repeated. The result was the creation of the enormous and costly Maginot Line, a vast system of interconnected fortresses, linked underground via railways, comprising barracks and hospitals, ammunition stores, and fuel and ventilation systems that would allow the forts to continue to function – and fight – even if surrounded by the enemy. At 7 billion French francs, the final cost of the line was far more than the original estimate.

The cost of construction and also the ongoing cost of maintenance inevitably meant that the funding available for other areas of the French armed forces was reduced greatly. Despite these considerations, however, there were few in France who would dispute the necessity of such an arrangement. Marshal Pétain summed up the French national faith in such defenses, referring to them as 'lavish

with steel, stingy with blood,' and after the horrors of the trenches, few disagreed.

There was a weakness in the whole arrangement, in that the line did not extend the length of the Franco-Belgian frontier – the obvious route for an invading army – and in fact stretched only from Strasbourg as far as Montmédy. The reasons for this were partly practical and partly economic as well as a reluctance to exclude Belgium from an alliance with France. If Belgium were left out of the Maginot Line, in all likelihood she would once again revert to her previous neutrality – she had been neutral in 1914 – and thereby provide a conduit for German aggression. In the event, Belgium opted for neutrality anyway, effectively scuppering French plans to move into prepared positions on Belgian soil. Similarly, the Maginot Line did not cover the area opposite the Ardennes, a densely wooded forest area, as it was considered to be 'impenetrable' to modern armored columns.

The sum total of these many considerations – a misplaced optimism in the strength of the Maginot Line, worries about the political position of Belgium, financial concerns, and an unwillingness to conceive that offensive, maneuver-type operations might hold the upper hand in a future war – all led to the development of what would be termed the 'Maginot mentality.' This amounted to a belief in the superiority of the defensive arrangement of the Maginot Line and an unwillingness to believe or acknowledge that warfare might have moved on.

The Maginot Line was also tremendously important for the Germans. Almost unwittingly, it had imposed upon the French a strategic straitjacket. There was little chance that, having shackled herself so firmly (and expensively) to the defensive, France was likely to go onto the attack. In 1935 the French Minister of War, in a speech to the French Chamber of Deputies, asserted: 'How can we still believe in the offensive when we have spent thousands of millions to establish a fortified barrier? Would we be mad enough to advance beyond this barrier upon goodness knows what adventure!'

Not only had the French national mentality become inextricably wedded to the defensive – a mindset both created and reinforced by the Maginot Line – but there were also other practical considerations. The Maginot Line had been the product of tremendous investment in defense budgets and manpower. With the Maginot Line receiving so much of the available moneys for defense, it severely restricted other areas of defense spending. Even had the French army not been so deficient in the means to adopt offensive operations, the means to fund new equipment to that end was absent. The knowledge of this would obviously aid Adolf Hitler, who was reasonably secure that, whatever action he might take in the east, it was highly unlikely that France would threaten seriously the western border of the Reich.

The French army in the 1930s suffered from a number of problems, many of them reflected in French life more widely. French troops were underpaid and undervalued, and the army was riven by many of the social and political divisions of the country at large. The French army continued to rely on telephone communication rather than radio. Similarly, the French failed to take on board the new potential of tanks. The French army of 1918 did not manage to enact the all-arms battle with any degree of conviction, generally reducing its tanks to the role of infantry support vehicles that were the means to the end of an infantry breakthrough. This was despite developing some excellent vehicles toward the end of the war. The French all-arms battle generally geared the speed of the other elements down to that of the slowest component, the infantry, rather than seeking to motorize the infantry and allow them to maintain the speed of the armored elements. Despite the protestations of a few French officers during the interwar period, notably those of Charles de Gaulle, French doctrine remained stubbornly behind the times.

Belgium

The small Belgian army had played as active a role as it could during the First World War and in the aftermath made serious efforts to preserve its security. The Belgians signed defensive agreements with both Britain and France and endeavored to maintain a large standing army, courtesy of conscription. However, by 1926 this commitment to a reasonably strong standing army had largely been abandoned and a reliance on the inevitability of British and French support in the event of war informed Belgium's defense posture. The advent of Hitler in 1933 prompted a renewal of Belgian military spending and by the time of the Anglo-French declaration of war, the Belgian army stood at nearly 600,000 men. The Belgian army, despite a number of modern and effective weapons, planned to fight a defensive war in the event of her neutrality, reaffirmed with the Anglo-French declaration of war on Germany being breached.

Poland

The Poles were to have the dubious distinction of being Hitler's first military victims. The performance of the Polish army in the early battles of the Second World War has attracted considerable attention, if only for the apparent futility of its desperate efforts to repel the German invaders. The

history of the Polish army is an interesting one. Poland, as an independent political entity, had effectively been off the map for the 123 years before 1918. Successive 'partitions' of Poland between Prussia, Imperial Russia, and the Austro-Hungarian Empire came to an end in 1918 when Poland was restored by the Treaty of Versailles, at the territorial expense of those same states.

Large numbers of Poles fought in the First World War, serving, ironically, in the armies of Germany, Russia, and also Austria-Hungry. It was the formations of Polish Legions raised by the Austro-Hungarians that were to have the largest and most disproportionate impact on the new army of independent Poland. A fledgling Polish army was soon established in the new Poland under the command of Jozef Pilsudski, the former commander of the Polish Legions in the Austrian army. Despite the unpromising origins of this essentially disparate, 'rag-tag' grouping, the Polish army was to score a notable success. The Poles were bolstered by a number of additional Polish formations, most notably the 'Haller' army, a formation of 25,000 Polish-American volunteers.

In the aftermath of the First World War and with the large empires of east and

Polish cavalry. (Topham Picturepoint)

Polish tankettes. (Steve Zaloga)

central Europe collapsing, there followed a general free-for-all as many states struggled to seize territory and incorporate ethnic kin within the boundaries of the new states. The Poles, emboldened by a number of local victories against the new masters of Russia, the Bolsheviks, joined with Ukrainian nationalist forces to invade the Ukraine and fight the Red Army. After the Poles enjoyed initial successes, the Red Army forced them all the way back to the gates of Warsaw. Then Pilsudski achieved an enormous reversal of Polish fortunes and defeated the Red Army so decisively that the Bolsheviks were obliged to conclude a humiliating peace settlement, something that rankled through the 1920s and 1930s and certainly contributed to Stalin's willingness to dismember the country in 1939.

Poland's strategic position was unpromising. Sandwiched between two powerful enemies, the Soviet Union to the east and Germany to the west, the nightmare scenario for Poland was, of course, a two-front war. Poland's strategic predicament was the source of considerable concern to Polish planners. In 1921 they managed to secure a defensive alliance with France. This obliged the French to assist the Poles in the event of Germany entering into a conflict that was already in progress between the Poles and Russia. If this criterion were fulfilled, France would attack Germany. This treaty had obvious benefits for the French, whose diplomatic maneuvering in the interwar years was directed toward containing and restricting

Germany. The Poles also secured a treaty with the Romanians that promised help against Russia rather than Germany.

The Treaty of Locarno, signed in 1925 between Britain, France and Weimar Germany, appeared to be a source of future trouble for Poland, guaranteeing as it did the frontiers of *western* Europe. The obvious problem lay in the fact that Germany, with her western borders secure from her most vehement enemy, France, might take the opportunity to redress some of her many territorial grievances in the east. In a masterstroke of diplomatic collusion, Hitler agreed a nonaggression pact between Germany and Poland.

Despite the judgement of history on the Polish army in the war with Germany, that it was fighting a thoroughly modern opponent with nineteenth-century tactics and equipment, the Polish army was in fact wedded to a doctrine of maneuver. These tactics were born of the successes and experiences of the fast-moving Russo-Polish War, but unfortunately while the ideas were modern, the means by which they were to be realized were most definitely from a bygone era. While the German ideas of maneuver utilized tanks, armored infantry, and self-propelled artillery, the Poles still placed their faith in cavalry and infantry marching on foot. The resulting clash could have only one winner.

'I have determined on a solution by force'

The Second World War began, effectively, with the German invasion of Poland. This event, in itself, might have been a comparatively local incident. What was required to turn it into a wider European war and a world war was the participation of Britain and France, which had both pledged to come to Poland's aid in the event of overt German aggression. The reasons why the British and French found themselves in this position may be traced to several years previously.

German territorial ambitions

Hitler intended to restore German power and prestige in Europe. To do so he first believed that it was necessary to secure the restitution of the territory and people that Germany had been obliged to give up under the terms of the Versailles settlement in 1919. Once all Germans had been incorporated into a Germany that itself encompassed traditional German territory, Hitler then had more ambitious plans. He intended that Germany should dominate Europe and conceived of such a situation in distinctly Darwinian terms. The Aryan Germans would demonstrate their superiority over races, such as the Slavs of eastern Europe, through war in a 'survival of the fittest' contest.

Hitler believed that a people must either expand or die and the area of expansion for the German superstate was to be in the east. The Slavic inhabitants of eastern Europe were to be reduced to a slave race, living openly to serve their German masters. The land conquered in the east would be colonized by Germans and would provide sufficient space for expansion (*Lebensraum*), something not available in Germany herself. Some peoples, the Jews and the gypsies for

example, were not considered fit enough even to serve the Germans and were to be eliminated. Writing in *Mein Kampf*, Hitler made the following declaration:

The foreign policy of a nation state must assure the existence on this planet of a race ... by creating a healthy, life-giving and natural balance between the present and future numbers of the Volk [people] on the one hand and, on the other, the quantity and quality of its territory.

With the reoccupation of the Rhineland in 1936, it was obvious that Hitler was intent on addressing Germany's territorial grievances. Hitler ordered the army into the Rhineland against the better judgement of his generals, and the German success there persuaded him of both his own infallibility in such matters and the weakness and indifference of his likely opponents, Britain and France.

Anschluss

Union with Austria was another important step for Hitler. Although forbidden by the Treaty of Versailles, it also ran counter to the ideas of self-determination enshrined in the treaty itself, as many Germans living in Austria did not want to be incorporated into Germany. Hitler, however, was extremely keen to bring the Germans in Austria within the greater Reich, not only for racial reasons, but also because Austria was the land of his birth.

In 1934 the Austrian Nazi Party had been banned by the then Austrian Chancellor, Dollfuss. Later that year, the Austrian Nazis attempted a coup d'état, but Hitler was persuaded not to intervene when Mussolini threatened to intervene on Dollfuss's behalf.

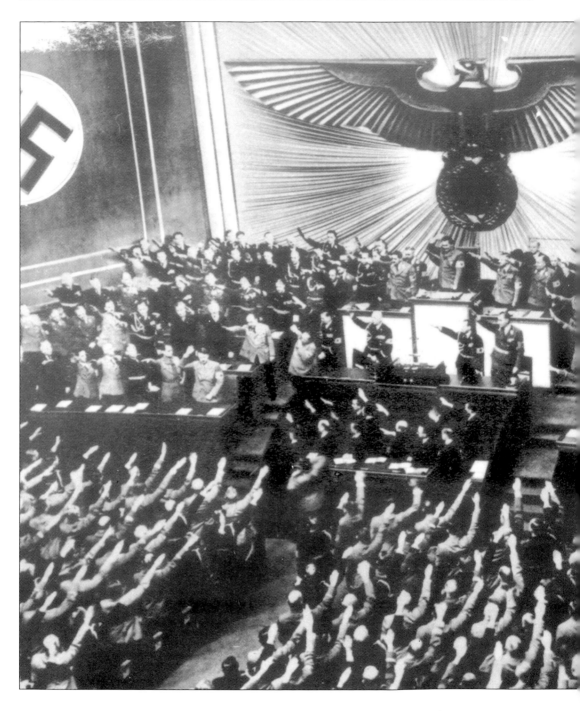

News of the *Anschluss* reaches the Reichstag. (Topham Picturepoint)

Four years later, following an improvement in Italian–German relations, with the announcement of the Rome–Berlin Axis and the more formal Anti-Comintern Pact, the Austrian Nazis began agitating again. At this juncture the Austrian Chancellor promised a plebiscite on Austria's future. Hitler was not confident that Austrians would vote to join Germany and this possibility forced his hand. Threatened with a German invasion, the government of Austria capitulated. In

For many in the outside world, the enforced separation of the ethnically similar Austrians and Germans was artificial and inappropriate. When Germany and Austria were united in what became known as the *Anschluss*, many observers dismissed Hitler's aggression on these grounds. But if they believed that this success would assuage rather than fuel his ambitions, they were certainly wrong.

The Sudetenland

Hitler's next concern was the future of the large numbers of Germans in Czechoslovakia, almost all of whom, unlike the Austrians, wished to be incorporated into Germany. The wholly artificial Czechoslovakian state had been constituted out of the former Austro-Hungarian Empire and German territory, and contained around 3 million ethnic Germans, living in that area of Czechoslovakia called the Sudetenland.

Since 1933, elements of the German minority in Czechoslovakia had been agitating for political autonomy from their ostensible parent nation, Czechoslovakia. They were led by a Nazi sympathizer, Konrad Henlein. There was some sympathy for the demands of the Sudeten Germans: after all, the right of self-determination had been enshrined in the Treaty of Versailles and what this minority wished for was, ostensibly, little different. At the 1938 Nazi Party rally in Nuremberg, Hitler made the following announcement, clearly demonstrating his ambitions over the future of the Sudeten Germans:

I believe that I shall serve peace best if I leave no doubt upon this point. I have not put forward the demand that Germany may oppress three and a half million Frenchmen or that, for instance, three and a half million of the English should be given up to us for oppression; my demand is that the oppression of three and a half million Germans in Czechoslovakia shall cease and that its place shall be taken by the

February 1938 the Austrian Chancellor, Schuschnigg, resigned and was replaced by the Nazi Seyss-Inquart, who invited in German troops. On 13 March he officially decreed Austria out of existence and Adolf Hitler became the Chancellor of a Greater Germany.

A poster advertising the plebiscite in the Sudetenland.
(AKG Berlin)

*free right of self-determination. We should be
sorry if, through this, our relations to the other
European states should be troubled or suffer
damage. But in that case the fault would not lie
with us.*

While the British Prime Minister, Neville
Chamberlain, appeared genuinely to believe
in Hitler's sincerity, the truth was that the
British and French were ill prepared for war.
When Hitler moved German troops to the
Czech border in early September, there
appeared to be every likelihood that
Germany would invade. However, Hitler was
reasonably sure that he could obtain what he
wanted through diplomacy and that the
British and French were unwilling to fight
for Czechoslovakia.

The British and French faced a number of
problems with regard to aiding
Czechoslovakia. The Czechs alone were
insufficiently strong to resist the Germans in
the event of war, and their most likely
supporters, the Soviet Union, could only send
aid by crossing Polish and Romanian territory,

Prelude to war: the Sudetenland, the Polish Corridor and Gleiwitz

1. German re-occupation of the Rhineland, May 1936.
2. Plebiscite in the Saarland, March 1935.
3. German occupation of Austria, March 1938.
4. Sudetenland given to Germany by Munich Agreement, September 1938.

something that the Poles and Romanians were unlikely to permit. In addition, the British and French were also uneasy about the prospect of Russian interference in Czechoslovakia. Although France and Czechoslovakia had a defensive agreement, there was consequently little will to fight, and even if there had been, Britain and France were too weak militarily to do so. The British and French therefore counseled the Czech leader Benes to agree to Hitler's demands and surrender the Sudetenland, even though this would entail the loss of the strategically most significant portion of Czechoslovakia and all her vital frontier fortifications, making any further German incursion a simple matter.

At a meeting on 15 September between Chamberlain and Hitler, at Hitler's mountain retreat of Berchtesgaden, Hitler revealed his intention to annex the Sudetenland under the principle of self-determination. After several days of escalating tension, during which time the Royal Navy prepared for war and France also began to mobilize, an agreement was reached to meet at Munich on 29 September. On 27 September, Chamberlain made this well-known comment:

How horrible, fantastic, incredible it is that we should be digging trenches and trying on gas masks here because of a quarrel in a far-away country between people of whom we know nothing. It seems still more impossible that a quarrel which has already been settled in principle should be the subject of war.

The Munich Conference, incredibly, did not feature a Czech representative, but instead Britain, France, Italy, and Germany met to decide the future of Czechoslovakia. Hitler signed an agreement promising that once the Sudetenland was transferred to Germany, the remaining Czech frontiers would be respected. After this Chamberlain flew back to England, landing at Croydon airport, and waved his famous piece of paper, signed by Hitler, which Chamberlain said guaranteed 'peace in our time.' On 15 March 1939, German troops entered the Czech capital, Prague, and occupied the Czech provinces of Bohemia and Moravia.

The Munich Conference. Left to right: Neville Chamberlain, Daladier, Adolf Hitler, Benito Mussolini, Count Gano (Ann Ronan Picture Library)

Chamberlain at Croydon after the Munich conference.
(Topham Picturepoint)

The Munich Conference of September 1938 has become shorthand for weakness in the face of obvious aggression and synonymous with the term 'appeasement.' Appeasement is an oft-heard term, but in this context it was the means by which the British and French in particular sought to pacify Hitler by agreeing to as many of his demands as possible in the hope of assuaging his ambition and, fundamentally, avoiding war. In fact the Munich Conference marked the end of appeasement and both Chamberlain and the French Prime Minister, Edouard Daladier, knew that rearmament must continue at a pace, as Hitler had only been temporarily satiated.

Poland

The final act that escalated local disputes into a major European and ultimately a world war was the German invasion of Poland. Following Hitler's move against the rump state of Czechoslovakia, the British government offered a military guarantee to Poland, intending to demonstrate to Hitler that a repetition of Munich would not be countenanced. This was also a recognition of the popular mood in Britain, where a measure of conscription was also introduced. Britain offered similar guarantees to both Romania and Greece, thereby reversing the longstanding pledge of previous British governments not to tie Britain into another continental commitment.

Hitler wanted Poland as the first major step toward obtaining *Lebensraum* in the east. The pretext was an obvious one: Germany proper was separated from her easternmost province, East Prussia, by a strip of Polish territory. It was not difficult to accuse the Poles of interfering with German access to East Prussia. Similarly, in the free city of Danzig, local Nazis went about the familiar business of creating trouble and demanding that the city be incorporated into the Reich. Hitler then had ample pretext to begin putting pressure on the Polish government to cede territory to Germany, in

the same fashion as the Czechs had been obliged to do.

The strategic position changed dramatically in August with the surprise announcement of the Molotov–Ribbentrop Pact between Germany and the Soviet Union. This expedient alliance brought together the two countries that would be deadly foes in only a couple of years. Stalin realized this and sought to delay the German assault on his country as long as possible. He also rationalized that a deeper border with Germany would have benefits for the Soviets, and readily agreed to help Germany attack Poland on the understanding that the Soviets would gain half of Polish territory. This accommodation gave Hitler the confidence to risk war, secure in the knowledge that the Soviet Union would not attack even if Britain and France did. Britain made it very clear to Germany that she would come to Poland's aid if need be. Hitler, however, was committed.

In defiance of British and French warnings, Adolf Hitler ordered his forces to invade. In OKW Directive No. 1, issued by Hitler on the last day of August 1939, he asserted the following: 'Having exhausted all political possibilities of rectifying the intolerable situation on Germany's eastern frontier by peaceful means, I have decided to solve the problem by force.'

The event needed to turn this action into a major European conflict occurred at 11.15 am on 3 September 1939. At 9.00 am, just over three hours previously, the British Prime Minister had issued Germany with an ultimatum, demanding that unless Britain heard by 11.00 am that Germany was prepared to withdraw her troops from Poland then a state of war would exist between Great Britain and Germany. At 11.15 am Neville Chamberlain made his immortal speech informing the British people that 'no such undertaking has been received and that, consequently, this country is at war with Germany.' Britain's ally, France, issued a similar ultimatum at noon on 3 September. When the deadline for the Germans' reply to that ultimatum came and

The Supreme Commander of the Armed Forces

OKW/Wfa Nr 170/39g. K. Chiefs. Li   Berlin
MOST SECRET   31st August 1939

Senior Commanders only   8 copies
By hand of Officer only   COPY No....

Directive No. 1 for the Conduct of War

1. Now that the political possibilities of disposing by peaceful means of a situation on the Eastern Frontier which is intolerable for Germany has been exhausted, I have determined on a solution by force.

2 The attack on Poland is to be carried out in accordance with the preparation made for 'Fall Weiss', with the alterations which result, where the Army is concerned, from the fact that it has in the meantime almost completed its dispositions. Allotment of tasks and the operational targets remain unchanged. The date of attack – 1 September, 1939. Time of attack – 4.45 [inserted in red pencil]. This timing also applies to operations at Gydnia, the bay of Danzig and the Dirschau bridge.

3. In the West it is important that the responsibility of the opening of hostilities should rest unequivocally with England and France. Minor frontier violations will be dealt with locally for the time being. The neutrality of Holland, Belgium, Luxemburg, Switzerland, which we have assured, is to be strictly observed. The Western frontier will not be crossed by land without my explicit orders. This also applies to all acts of war at sea. Defensive measures by the Luftwaffe are to be restricted to repulsing firmly any enemy air attacks on the frontiers of the Reich. Care must be taken to respect the frontiers of neutral countries as far as possible, when countering single aircraft or small units. Only when large numbers of British or French bombers are employed against German territory across neutral territory, will the Air Force be allowed to fly counterattacks over the same neutral soil. It is especially important to keep the IKW informed of every infringement of neutral territory by our Western enemies.

4. Should England and France open hostilities against Germany then it will be the duty of the Armed Forces operating in the West, while conserving their strength as much as possible, to maintain conditions for the successful conclusion of operations against Poland. The order to commence offensive operations is reserved absolutely to me.

The Army will hold the West Wall and should take steps to secure it from being outflanked in the north, by any violation of Belgian or Dutch borders by the Western powers. Should the French invade Luxembourg, permission is given to blow the frontier bridges.

The Navy will operate against merchant shipping, with England as the focal point. Certain zones may be declared danger areas in order to increase the effectiveness of such measures. The OKM will report on these areas and will submit the text of a public declaration in this matter, which is to be drawn up in collaboration with the Foreign Office and submitted to me for approval via the OKW. The Baltic Sea is to be secured against enemy incursions. OKM will decide if it is necessary to mine the entrances to the Baltic for this purpose.

The Air Force is primarily to prevent French or English air forces attacking German land forces or German territory. In operations against England it is the task of the Luftwaffe to harrass England's important trade at sea, her armaments industry and the transport of troops to France. Any favourable opportunity to attack enemy naval concentrations, especially battleships and aircraft carriers, must be taken. Any decision to attack London rests with me. Attacks against the English home land should be prepared, bearing in mind that partial success with insufficient forces is to be avoided at all costs.

signed: **ADOLF HITLER**

(translated from the original in Part II of the Nuremberg Documents)

Directive No. 1 for the conduct of war, reproduced from *The Fall of France*, by G. Fortey and John Duncan (Tunbridge Wells, 1990).

went, at 5.00 pm that day, France too was once again at war with Germany.

The American journalist William Shirer, who wrote regular dispatches from Germany during the early years of the Second World War, had this to say about the reaction of the German people to the announcement that Germany would now face a war against the British and the French:

In 1914, I believe, the excitement in Berlin on the first day of the world war was tremendous. Today, no excitement, no hurrahs, no cheering, no throwing of flowers, no war fever, no war hysteria. There is not even any hate for the British and French – despite Hitler's various proclamations to the people, the Party, the East Army, the West Army, accusing the 'English warmongers and capitalistic Jews' of starting this war. When I passed the French and British embassies this afternoon, the sidewalk in front of each of them was deserted. A lone schupo [short for Schutzspolizei *or policeman] paced up and down before each.*

Whatever the average German might have felt about the war, there was now no way back.

Hitler strikes

The invasion of Poland

The invasion of Poland was the first strike in a total war. Hitler's new army was now to be tested on the field of combat against the large and well-trained armed forces of the Polish state – the same nation that had famously stopped the Red Army before Warsaw in 1920. As it turned out, however, the poignant and tragic imagery of Polish cavalry fighting against, and hopelessly outclassed by, German armor would prove to be one of the most significant and defining images of the war. The years of training and exercises that the German army had engaged in since 1919 were now to be put into practice with devastating effect.

German troops cross the border into Poland. (Ann Ronan Picture Library)

Despite Hitler's ambition and confidence, the Germans went through an elaborate charade in order to convince the world that Germany was provoked. Men from the *Sicherheitsdienst* or SD department of the SS, under the overall direction of Reinhard Heydrich, planned an operation to precipitate the war that Hitler wanted. This operation, code-named Hindenburg, involved three simultaneous raids: the first was on the radio station at Gleiwitz, the second on the small customs post at Hochlinden, and the third on an isolated gamekeeper's hut at Pitschen. The raids were to be conducted by men dressed in Polish uniforms, and at Gleiwitz the plan was that the attack would be heard live on radio – with the attackers' voices, speaking in Polish and declaiming Germany, being broadcast live over the air to maximize their impact.

Reinhard Heydrich, 1904–42 was chief of the SS and the
originator of the Final Solution plan. (Topham Picturepoint)

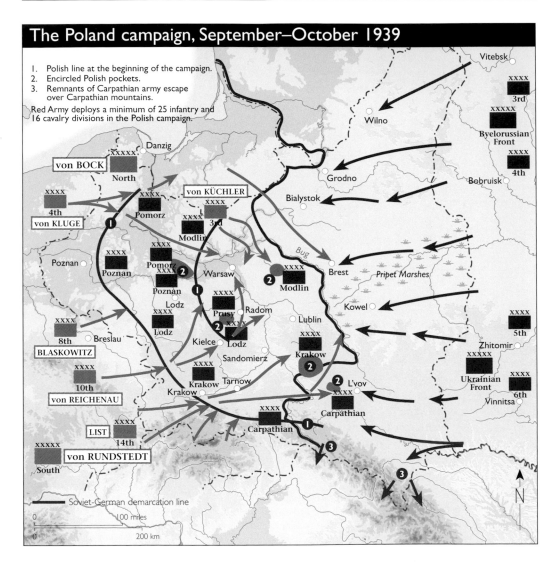

The Poland campaign, September–October 1939

1. Polish line at the beginning of the campaign.
2. Encircled Polish pockets.
3. Remnants of Carpathian army escape over Carpathian mountains.

Red Army deploys a minimum of 25 infantry and 16 cavalry divisions in the Polish campaign.

von BOCK — North
von KLUGE — 4th — Pomorz
von KÜCHLER — 3rd — Modlin
BLASKOWITZ — 8th — Breslau
von REICHENAU — 10th — Krakow
LIST — 14th
von RUNDSTEDT — South

Danzig, Poznan, Pomorz, Poznan, Lodz, Lodz, Kielce, Krakow, Tarnow, Krakow, Sandomierz, Carpathian, Carpathian

Grodno, Bialystok, Warsaw, Modlin, Brest, Pripet Marshes, Kowel, Lublin, Radom, Prusy, Krakow, L'vov, Carpathian

Wilno, Vitebsk, Byelorussian Front, 3rd, 4th, Bobruisk, Ukrainian Front, 5th, Zhitomir, 6th, Vinnitsa

Bug

Soviet–German demarcation line

0 — 100 miles
0 — 200 km

N

After a number of false starts and poor organization bordering on the farcical, the attacks took place. Four condemned men from the Sauchsenhausen concentration camp and a single German (a local Polish sympathizer) were murdered to provide evidence for the Polish incursions – the corpses, dressed in Polish uniforms, were photographed to complete the provocation. Despite the planning, the radio attack failed to be broadcast because of the poor strength of the transmitter. Hitler was nevertheless able to announce to the Reichstag on 1 September that 'Polish troops of the regular army have been firing on our territory during the night [of 31 August/1 September].

Since 05.45 we have been returning that fire.' The Second World War was up and running.

The German attack on Poland began on 1 September. The position was greatly aided by Hitler's successful 'annexation' of Czechoslovakia, as Poland was now situated uncomfortably between the twin prongs of German-held territory. To the east, Stalin's Red Army bided its time before, on 17 September, acting in accordance with the secret clauses of the Molotov–Ribbentrop Pact and also invading Poland. The Poles, caught between the forces of Nazi Germany and the Soviet Union, did not manage to maintain resistance for long.

The German plan for the invasion of Poland was termed *Fall Weiss* or 'Case White' and essentially aimed to defeat the Polish army by encircling and destroying Polish army formations. The Germans planned to do this at the tactical level, but also at the strategic level, with German sights focused upon Warsaw, the Polish capital. The Poles were outnumbered both in terms of modern tanks and also in terms of tactics. The Germans mobilized 50 divisions for the Polish campaign, including six Panzer divisions, four motorized divisions, and three mountain divisions. These sizable forces represented the bulk of the available German army, leaving only 11 divisions in the west, where the French army was 10 times that number.

The Germans deployed their armored formations in such a manner as to maximize the attributes of their Panzer troops, rapidly outflanking the slower-moving Poles and creating the conditions for the *Kesselschlachten*, or 'cauldron battles,' that the Germans were so keen to fight. These involved the rapid penetration of the enemy's defenses via the weakest spot, followed by the encirclement of the enemy. The enemy was therefore compelled either to stand and fight, suffering artillery and air bombardment, or to attempt a breakout, in which case it would be forced to relinquish the advantage conveyed by its prepared defensive positions.

The Germans made good progress across ground baked hard by the long, hot summer of 1939 and were aided also by their overwhelming air superiority, established within the opening three days by the vastly more impressive Luftwaffe. In a pattern that would be dreadfully familiar over the ensuing years, German aircraft struck at the Polish air force on the ground, effectively removing it from the equation. German aircraft flew hundreds of sorties in support of troops on the ground, operating essentially as an aerial dimension to the German army. While the Poles were acutely aware of the likelihood of the German military action and had reasonably good intelligence as to the growing concentrations of German forces, they were still taken by surprise when the attack actually happened. The Germans were able to seize the initiative and held it for the duration of what proved to be a depressingly short campaign.

Army Group North, comprising the 4th Army under Kluge and the 3rd Army under Kuchler, struck the first blow in the campaign. The two-army formation in East Prussia and Pomerania quickly overran the Polish Corridor and the free city of Danzig. Further to the south, Army Group South under the command of von Rundstedt had three army-sized formations, 8th Army (Blaskowitz), 10th Army (Reichenau), and 14th Army (List), which drove westwards into the heart of Poland. The Poles rallied briefly around the city of Poznan and succeeded in driving the Germans back, but this offered

German cavalry column in twos, possibly members of the 1st Cavalry Division. (IWM RML225)

only a brief respite and these Polish troops were eventually overrun. The Germans, courtesy of two encirclements (the second being required when the Poles withdrew faster than anticipated) were in a position by 16 September to have surrounded the bulk of Polish forces in western Poland. They were able to snap shut the pincers of their encircling operation at will.

By 16 September the German forces had the Polish capital, Warsaw, surrounded, and they proceeded to bombard the city from the air and the ground. Warsaw eventually surrendered on 27 September with around 40,000 civilian casualties. The Russian invasion of Poland on 17 September was the deathblow for Poland. Predictably, it met little or no resistance as the Poles were both taken completely by surprise and totally immersed in the fighting against German forces in the east of their country. The Polish General Staff had no plans for fighting a war on two fronts, east and west, simultaneously. In fact, the Poles had considered that it was impossible to wage a two-front war.

The timing of the Soviet assault was also of considerable surprise to Germany. Hitler had been attempting to persuade Stalin to enter the war against Poland for some time, reasoning that the western powers then might refrain from intervening at all (i.e. not declare war on Germany) or, if not, might declare war on the Soviet Union as well. Stalin, predictably, had his own agenda with regard to the hapless Polish state. Soviet forces refrained from entering the fighting in Poland while the Red Army organized and re-equipped.

When the Red Army finally crossed the border, it did so under the weak pretence that it was responding to alleged border violations and that the intervention was aimed purely at 'the protection of the Ukrainians and Belorussians, with full preservation of neutrality in the present conflict.' Stalin also asserted that, with no *effective* Polish government now in existence, the 'Soviet government is no longer bound by the provisions and demands of the Soviet–Polish non-aggression treaty,' and was therefore at liberty to enter the war against

its former ally. While the Soviets received little in the way of significant resistance from the Poles, they did engage in minor skirmishes with German troops whom they met on their advance. It took some time before the position was established and the German and Soviet formations respected the boundary line, which followed the course of the River Bug, along which the two unlikely allies had agreed to divide Poland.

On 19 September the Polish government left Warsaw and eventually established a government in exile. This government, under Wladyslaw Sikorski, finally settled in London after the fall of France. Besides the Polish leaders, many Polish servicemen also escaped, with some 90,000 making their way to France and Britain.

What were the key reasons for the rapid collapse of Poland? There are several. First, Poland's strategic situation was poor: with the conclusion of the Molotov–Ribbentrop Pact on 23 August 1939, Poland was effectively surrounded. The addition of the Soviet Union to the side of Germany compounded the territorial adjustments that had been wrought with Germany's successful dismemberment of Czechoslovakia. The surprise that characterized the German assault also prevented the Poles from doing a better defensive job. This, in combination with the new weaponry employed with such devastating effect by the Wehrmacht, left the Poles struggling to match the Germans, and with the invasion from the east by the Soviet Union, any hope of continuing the fight was effectively removed. Nevertheless, the Poles, for all the ultimate futility of their efforts, did manage to inflict significant casualties on the Germans. They destroyed in the region of 200 German tanks, about 10 percent of the total number deployed, and also killed 13,000 German soldiers, wounding a further 30,000.

The 'phoney war'

While Poland was fighting for her survival in the east, in the west her two allies, Britain and France, did nothing. Given that France and Britain had declared war on Germany because of the attack on Poland, and France and Britain were committed guarantors of Polish independence, this inaction seems strangely at odds. The British had successfully dispatched the British Expeditionary Force (BEF), numbering 140,000 men, to France by 30 September 1940, but even then no offensive action was contemplated.

Prior to this, on 7 September, elements of the French Fourth and Seventh Armies had advanced into Germany in the vicinity of Saarbrucken. This initial incursion reached no more than about 5 miles (8km) along a 16-mile (26km) front. German military formations in the area withdrew behind the Seigfried Line. At this point, the bulk of the German army was still in Poland and the *Daily Mail* in Britain ran a headline that claimed 'French Army pouring over the German border.' However, the French advance went no further, and following the Polish surrender, the French forces withdrew.

'It was only a token invasion. We did not wish to fight on their territory and we did not ask for this war,' a senior French officer was alleged to have said. Certainly, it was a fortuitous development for the Germans, who were surprised that the western allies did not make more of the strategic opportunity before them. After the war, the German Field Marshal, Keitel, commented that 'we were astonished to find only minor skirmishes undertaken between the Siegfried and the Maginot Lines. We did not understand why France did not seize this unique opportunity and this confirmed us in the idea that the Western Powers did not desire war against us.'

This period between the Anglo-French declaration of war and the fall of France is known as the 'phoney war' because of the very inaction of both sides. The Germans were honing their plans for the assault on the Allies in the west, and the Allies too were busying themselves with organizing their counter-effort. The BEF dug what was known as the 'Gort' Line (after General The

Viscount Gort, the commanding officer of the BEF) and civilians back in Britain also dug air-raid trenches and prepared for the air war that most thought would come.

The Russo-Finnish War

Elsewhere in Europe, more bitter fighting began with the outbreak of the Russo–Finnish War. This conflict has rarely received the coverage it perhaps deserves, peripheral as it was to the larger picture. Nonetheless, some important lessons were learnt from it. The war is known more commonly as the 'Winter War' and ran from 30 November until 13 March 1940, during which time Stalin's ill-advised thrust into his near neighbor's territory resulted in a bloody nose for the Red Army.

The Red Army, in November 1939, was a far cry from the powerful and well-organized force that would eventually defeat Hitler's Germany. In fact, in the Winter War against Finland, the Soviets proved remarkably inept. Their difficulties against the Finns, in combination with the purges of the 1930s, probably persuaded Hitler that the Red Army was not likely to prove a formidable opponent in the future. Certainly the Germans were to underestimate the courage and tenacity of the ordinary Soviet soldier when they eventually invaded the Soviet Union in June 1941.

In October 1939, flush from the success of the limited campaign in Poland, Stalin issued an ultimatum to the Finnish government demanding a redrawing of the Russo-Finnish border north of Leningrad, in the Karelian peninsula. The Finns, who had only won independence from Russian dominance in 1917, declined and a short, bitter war ensued. The Finns outfought their numerically superior opponents, using hit-and-run tactics and making the best use of the terrain and climate to thwart Soviet intentions. By January 1940, however, the Soviet attack had been stabilized and the Red Army began to employ its strengths in a more effective fashion.

A scene from the Russo-Finnish War. (Topham Picturepoint)

The Finns eventually sued for peace in March 1940 and were obliged to concede the territorial demands originally required of them in October 1939. The Finns suffered roughly 25,000 casualties, but the Red Army came off far worse. Around 200,000 Red Army soldiers were lost in Finland, many through exposure. The Red Army, however, had learnt some valuable lessons for the future.

Hostilities resumed between the Finns and the Soviet Union during what became known as the 'Continuation War' of 1941–44 when the Finns formally allied themselves to Germany. The Finnish leader, Mannerheim, skillfully detached himself from the Germans when their defeat became evident. Although his terms for peace with the Soviet Union meant a permanent acknowledgment of the border situation of spring 1940, Mannerheim's actions did at least ensure that his country did not fall under the sway of the Soviet Union, as did so many other states at the war's end.

The Norway campaign

While the western allies were content to bide their time in France, in Norway they at last took the offensive. The Allied campaign in Norway was to prove a fascinating mix of strategic ineptitude coupled with extraordinary individual heroism. The German economy was reliant on over 10 million tons of iron ore each year being imported from Sweden. The route of this vital component was overland from Sweden to Norway and thence from the Norwegian port of Narvik to Germany. If the Allies could

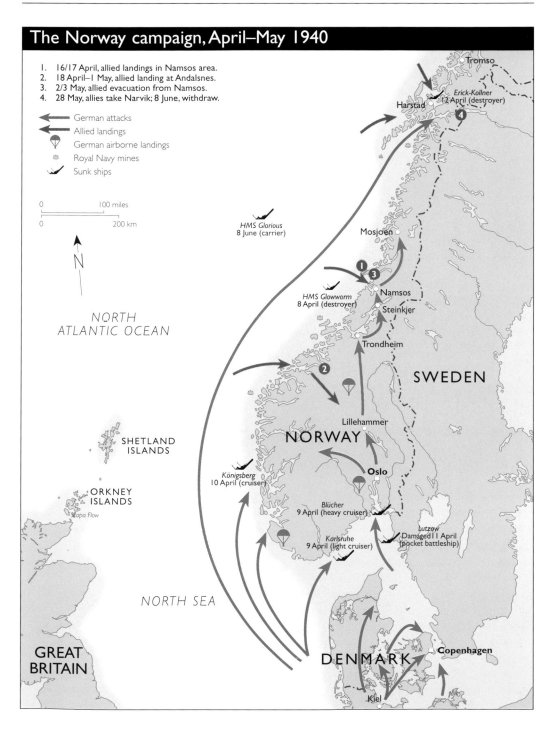

The Norway campaign, April–May 1940

1. 16/17 April, allied landings in Namsos area.
2. 18 April–1 May, allied landing at Andalsnes.
3. 2/3 May, allied evacuation from Namsos.
4. 28 May, allies take Narvik; 8 June, withdraw.

- German attacks
- Allied landings
- German airborne landings
- Royal Navy mines
- Sunk ships

0   100 miles
0   200 km

Tromso

Erick-Kollner
12 April (destroyer)

Harstad

HMS Glorious
8 June (carrier)

Mosjoen

NORTH
ATLANTIC OCEAN

HMS Glowworm
8 April (destroyer)

Namsos
Steinkjer

Trondheim

SWEDEN

Lillehammer

NORWAY

SHETLAND
ISLANDS

Königsberg
10 April (cruiser)

Oslo

Blücher
9 April (heavy cruiser)

ORKNEY
ISLANDS

Scapa Flow

Karlsruhe
9 April (light cruiser)

Lutzow
Damaged 11 April
(pocket battleship)

NORTH SEA

GREAT
BRITAIN

DENMARK   Copenhagen

Kiel

prevent the regular flow of ore, they would inflict a crucial blow against Germany's war effort. There was also some discussion of providing aid to the Finns in their struggle against the Soviets, and the easiest route to do this would be across Norway.

The Germans too were concerned at this vulnerability and resolved to take Norway, which would also provide bases for German surface vessels and submarines. First, however, German forces struck at Denmark. The Danes were ill prepared for a war against

German troops at the Polar circle in Norway. (AKG Berlin).

their powerful neighbor and the Danish government ordered that no resistance should be put up against the invading Germans. Denmark formally surrendered on the same day as the German invasion, 9 April 1940.

The Norwegians, however, were determined to put up a fight. Joining them were 12,000 British and French troops, originally earmarked to join the Finns in their battle against the Soviets. The Finnish capitulation meant that these Allied forces could endeavor to engage the Germans in Norway. Prompt action by the Germans meant that their invasion force landed first, at Oslo, Bergen, Stavanger, and Kristiansand. Fierce Norwegian resistance gave the Allies time and an Allied force landed in the vicinity of Trondheim, from where it engaged German forces heading north from Oslo. Despite success by the Royal Navy

against the German Navy, bad planning and confusion blighted the whole operation. After six weeks of fighting, the Allied troops were outfought and eventually evacuated on 8 June. The Norwegian government escaped to Britain and the Germans installed a puppet government under the Norwegian Vidkun Quisling.

France and the Low Countries

Having dealt with the Poles and secured Germany's eastern borders from the threat of attack by the Soviet Union, courtesy of the Molotov–Ribbentrop Pact, Hitler was finally able to deal with France. What was to happen now would astonish the world and turn traditional ideas of strategy and tactics on their head. To gain some idea of what the German armed forces managed to achieve in their invasion of France and the Low Countries, it is useful to draw a parallel with the First World War. Between 1914 and 1918 the armed forces of Imperial Germany had striven to defeat the combined forces of Britain and France. In four years they failed to achieve this aim and in doing so also suffered over 2 million dead as well as experiencing a revolution that swept away the Kaiser and all remnants of the overseas empire that he had tried so hard to establish. Now, in the spring of 1940, Adolf Hitler's new Germany would deal the western allies a crippling blow and achieve in five weeks, and for the loss of only 13,000 killed, what the armies of the Kaiser had not achieved in four years.

The eventual German plan of attack was arrived at only by much discussion and the intervention of fate as well as by judgement. The initial German plan was an uninspired repetition of the German advance of August 1914 and was based upon an invasion of Belgium. This operation, essentially a rerun of the Schlieffen Plan, was known as Case Yellow or *Fall Gelb*. The plan was a cautious one and reflected in part the concerns that many senior German officers had over the latent potential of the French army. Case Yellow would see German forces making a frontal assault on the Allied positions in Belgium and the Low Countries and a smaller, diversionary thrust of German forces through the densely wooded and seemingly impenetrable Ardennes region. The Allied response to this probable thrust was the Dyle Plan, which had the best French units and the BEF advancing into Belgium and Holland, thereby avoiding fighting in northern France as well as meeting the German advance.

This plan was not to last for long as the principal means of German advance. Hitler was not keen on the plan, believing that the potential for the German forces to stall and then become bogged down was too great. Hitler's vacillation over the plan was hastened by the crash landing, on 9 January, of a Luftwaffe aircraft with a German paratroops officer on board near Mechelen, in Belgium. In his possession was a copy of Case Yellow, the officer in question having

been on his way to a conference in Cologne from his base in Münster. Although efforts were made to destroy the plans, enough remained of the documents to make it all too obvious that the Germans intended to strike at France, once again, through Belgium.

Once aware of the German intentions, the Allies changed the original Dyle Plan using a modification, known as the Breda variant, which called for the Allies to advance to the line of the Dyle River and also commit the bulk of their reserves. However, the capture of the German plans did nothing more than reinforce in the minds of the Allied generals, and the French Commander-in-Chief General Maurice Gamelin in particular, that their original assumptions about the likely German approach were correct.

The German response to the capture of the details of Case Yellow was also interesting. Hitler, as we have seen, was less than enthusiastic about the original idea and had some notions of his own about how to proceed. Simultaneously, and independently, General Erich von Manstein had been working on how to improve Case Yellow. The new plan, sometimes called the Manstein Plan, called for an audacious switch of effort, with the original, diversionary, thrust through the Ardennes now to be the main point of attack.

While the Ardennes was considered by most, the western allies included, to be 'impassable,' this was not the case. The Ardennes region did not have wide roads and was heavily wooded, with many streams and rivers. Despite this, it was passable, albeit slowly and with some difficulty. However, moving a formation the size that the Manstein plan envisaged through the narrow roads would be a tremendous gamble and would require a sophisticated deception plan and coordinated air support to ensure that the passage was neither discovered nor interdicted.

The Manstein Plan required Army Group A to effect a passage through the Ardennes, cross the River Meuse, and break out into the ideal tank country beyond. The formation

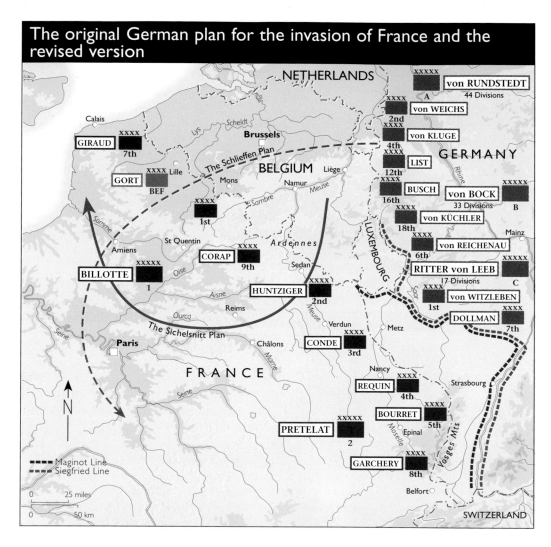

The original German plan for the invasion of France and the revised version

that was to have shouldered the original burden of the main thrust, Army Group B, was now to attack the Low Countries. Army Group B was to defeat the Dutch and Belgian forces while ensuring that the large numbers of quality British and French troops were 'fixed' to prevent them from acting against the main German effort. German aircraft were also tasked with ensuring that the Allies were kept well away from the Ardennes. The role of Army Group B in the north was crucial and likened to that of 'the matador's cloak,' a target tempting enough to persuade the Allied bull to engage it. Army Group C, further south, was to carry out a deception plan opposite the Maginot Line so as to confuse matters still further.

In March 1940, Hitler approved this plan, with additional embellishments from General Franz Halder. The role of Army Group B, the deception formation, has traditionally been given scant attention amidst the dynamic and audacious activities of the other German formations. However, the Germans themselves set a great deal of store by the deception plans in the north, designed not necessarily to change opinions of where the main effort of German activity would fall, but rather to confirm in the minds of senior Allied officers what they themselves had erroneously concluded.

The French wished, essentially, to recreate the Great War's set-piece battles of attrition, but they also wished to reverse the roles. In the French mind, it was the Germans who would be launching futile and costly attacks on well-defended French positions. The French had put considerable faith in the impressive fortifications of the Maginot Line, named after its instigator, the Defense Minister André Maginot. This interconnected line of fortifications stretched the length of the Franco-German border and was well nigh impregnable. The French did not believe that the Germans were likely to attempt to batter their way through. Instead the value of the Maginot Line was that it obliged any German invasion to come through Belgium, most probably in a repeat of the 1914 Stilton Plan, and thus defensive arrangements could be planned to deal with the threat along this predictable axis of advance.

The Allied strategy was essentially a long-term one: to draw the Germans into the

Panzerkampfwagen III Ausf. F, shown here in Yugoslavia in 1941. (US National Archives)

type of fighting that had worked so well between 1914 and 1918, that of fixed positions with an emphasis on attrition, hopefully wearing down the Germans in a fashion similar to the First World War. The Germans were aware of this and were determined that such a situation should not arise. Hitler knew the trenches of the First World War only too well and was determined to avoid a repetition. He sought to conduct a rapid campaign that would end the war quickly before its demands could overburden the German economy – itself not configured for a prolonged war. However, the German method of war fighting, too, was not without its weaknesses.

On 10 May 1940, German forces attacked the Low Countries Belgium, Holland, and Luxembourg. That same day the British Prime Minister, Chamberlain, resigned and Winston Churchill took over. Churchill's accession to power, however, could not stop the subsequent events. As well as

achieving their strategic aims in short order – the destruction of France and the isolation of Britain – the Germans did so by employing the experience they had gained in the Polish campaign to even more devastating effect.

It was after the France campaign that Germany's devastatingly effective tactics became firmly associated with *Blitzkrieg*, the term subsequently being misappropriated by dozens of historians and generals as a byword for fast, effective armored warfare. In fact, the term *Blitzkrieg* is one that would have thoroughly mystified German soldiers – officers and men alike – prior to 1940. It is not to be found in any German field manuals or army correspondence dealing with the conduct of operations. Rather, the term was mentioned first by an Italian journalist who used it to describe the type

The British Vickers Mark VI used in light cavalry units was under-armored and under-gunned when compared to its German counterparts. (The Tank Museum, Bovington)

of fighting that he had seen in France and the Low Countries.

Crucially, then, *Blitzkrieg* is descriptive rather than prescriptive and was coined to describe what the German tactics did rather than the more elusive notion of how they did it. There was a good reason for this. The Germans themselves were not entirely sure that what they were doing was new at all. In fact, to a great extent the practices of fast thrust, encirclement, and then annihilation of the encircled troops were not new at all but had been practiced by German (and Prussian) armies for years before, and by other armies as well.

What was really new in 1940 was the way the Germans were achieving their fast thrusts to encircle their opponents. Whereas in 1870, against the French, the Prussians would have used cavalry, now the Wehrmacht deployed tanks. Of course, the Germans were not the only state to possess tanks. Unlike in the Polish campaign, with its heroic but tragic mismatches of Polish cavalry against German armor, the British

The French Char B1 tank was an impressive vehicle but its effectiveness was hampered by the penny-packet fashion with which it was employed.

and French were well provided with tanks. Also, contrary to popular perceptions about this phase of the war, if anything the tanks of the British and the French were of better quality than the German vehicles and certainly were not inferior.

However, while Britain had taken the lead in the conception and development of tanks in the First World War, and indeed had employed them in the most innovative and successful fashion of all the major combatants in the Great War, this lead had largely evaporated in the interwar years. Germany, despite the limitations imposed on her by the Versailles settlement, had conducted exercises with mock-tanks, sure in the knowledge that the tank would prove to be a major element on the battlefield.

Numerically, the French army on its own had more tanks than the Germans were able to field, which meant that when French tanks were combined with those deployed as part of the BEF, the western allies had a marked numerical superiority: 3,383 tanks deployed compared to Germany's 2,445. Numbers alone, however, are rarely the deciding factor in combat; obviously the quality of the equipment is also of vital significance. Here too the Anglo-French forces were not embarrassed. The French were equipped with a variety of tanks, the best of which were the Somua S35 and the Char B. These were more than a match for the German Panzer IIs and IIIs with which the majority of the German Panzer formations were armed. The Panzer divisions were equipped with 1,400 Marks I and II; 349 Mark IIIs, with a 37mm (1.5-inch) gun; and only 278 of the larger, 24-ton Mark IVs, armed with a far more substantial

The Battle of France: opening moves

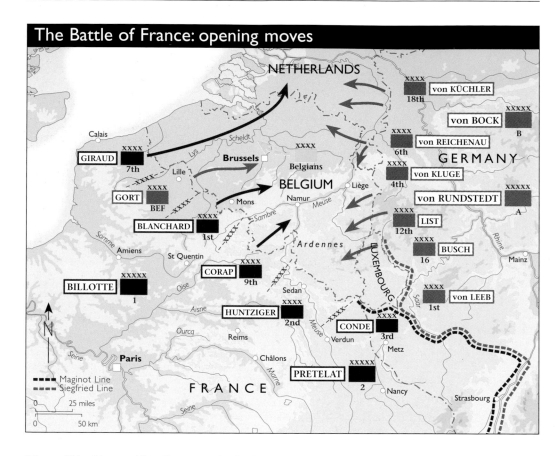

75mm (3-inch) gun. The Germans also had a number of excellent Czech-built tanks, a result of Germany's earlier takeover of that country.

In other areas, the French superiority was marked. The French army possessed far more artillery than the Germans, for example, fielding in the region of 11,000 pieces compared to the Germans' 8,000. But the Germans, although numerically weaker, did have mobile artillery: self-propelled pieces that equipped units deployed with Panzer divisions. These enabled them to be used in a far more dynamic and effective fashion than the static role favored by the French.

The Germans went to considerable lengths to convince the Allies that the main blow would come in the north. Airborne forces attacked bridges spanning the Mass, Waal, and Lek rivers, and cut the Netherlands in two. Parachute engineers also attacked the impressive Belgian fortress of Eben Emael, the linchpin of Belgium's defenses. In a move of

brilliant audacity, the German Paras negated all of Eben Emael's strengths. The fort was virtually impregnable from attack on the ground, such was the thickness of its walls. The Germans negated these strengths by landing on the roof of the fortress, using gliders that made no sound, and thus denied the defenders the opportunity to react earlier. The German troops blasted their way into the fortress and held it until relieved.

While Army Group B continued with its operations, further south, Army Group A penetrated the Ardennes. The Luftwaffe flew innumerable sorties on the first few days to protect the long and slow Panzer columns, terribly vulnerable in the narrow confines of the Ardennes roads. This was the Allies' main chance: if the advance of Army Group A had been spotted in time and sufficient force brought to bear, the outcome of the campaign would have been totally different. Instead, only light Allied air attacks threatened the German advance. The

German troops crossing the River Meuse in rubber
boats (Ian Baxter)

Germans encountered only moderate
resistance on the ground, mainly from
reserve formations, and this proved
insufficient to prevent the advance of the
Panzers – seven divisions all told. By the
evening of 12 May, these units had reached
the east bank of the River Meuse. The
German forces now demonstrated that they
possessed a host of attributes.

On 13 May the Germans successfully
crossed the Meuse at Dinant, courtesy of a
weir left intact by the French. Further south,
at the town of Sedan, German infantry and
combat engineers crossed the river at
astonishing speed under cover of a
concentrated air and artillery barrage.
German infantry established a foothold on
the western bank and within hours pontoon
bridges were constructed across the river and
Panzers began to cross. The all-arms
combination functioned perfectly, with all
the participating units knowing the aim of
their mission and all working in concert to
achieve it.

By the morning of 16 May, over
2,000 German tanks and in excess of
150,000 German troops had crossed the
River Meuse along a 50-mile (80km) stretch.
This breach of the Allied defensive line
effectively sealed the fate of the Allied armies
in northwest France and the Low Countries,
and paved the way for the decisive, strategic
success of the German assault. The German
formations, now in open country, began
their drive for the Channel in a
northwesterly arc, deep into the rear areas of
the British and French formations deployed
in Belgium.

The opportunity for the Allies to defeat
the apparently inevitable German advance,
however, was considerable. The German
lines of communication were by necessity
very extended, stretching back to the Meuse

Blown bridge over the River Meuse. (Ann Ronan Picture Library)

and beyond. These extended lines of communication were as much a feature of the German *Blitzkrieg* as anything and were a real vulnerability in the German methods of war fighting. Here was an opportunity for the Anglo-French to drive across the 'Panzer corridor' and regain some of the initiative.

If, as seems to be the case, there was not a massive gulf between the quality of the German armored formation and their Anglo-French opponents, nor was there a discrepancy in numbers between the Germans and the western allies. Indeed, the Anglo-French forces were able to field more armored vehicles than the Germans. How, then, can we explain the apparently overwhelming success of the Germans? Fundamentally it came down to the way in which armor was employed by the respective sides. The Allies used their tanks in small formations – what was known as 'penny-packets' – and as, in effect, little more than infantry support weapons rather than as weapons with an intrinsic, dynamic potential of their own. The BEF was almost completely mobile – the only participating army that could make such a claim. Yet, the British failed to make the most of this capability.

Other considerations did mark out German Panzers from their Allied counterparts. While armor and gun and speed might have been equal amongst the respective sides, the Germans had one crucial advantage. Most of the individual Panzers were equipped with radios. On the Allied side, only 20 percent of tanks were similarly equipped. It has been said elsewhere that the key technical development in the evolution of *Blitzkrieg* involved neither the tank nor the aircraft – both of which acquired in the 1930s the reliability, range, and speed needed for deep penetration operations – but the miniaturization of the radio. General Guderian had received his initial experience of combat as an officer in a signals unit, and his appreciation of the need for effective communication was vital. The miniature radio enabled the tanks to be used to maximum effect and facilitated the interaction between the armored formations and other branches or arms of the German armed forces.

The Germans also practiced their ideas of *Auftragstaktic* to a far greater extent in France and this was well served by the abundance of radios. The British and especially the French were nowhere near as up to date and were often suspicious of radio communications because of their susceptibility to interception. Von Kluge, Commander of the German 4th Army, summed up the importance of mission command in the German war-fighting method:

The most important facet of German tactics remained the mission directive, allowing subordinates the maximum freedom to accomplish their assigned task. That freedom of action provided tactical superiority over the more schematic and textbook approach employed by the French and English.

The following quotation from a 3 Panzer Division Report (1940) also stresses the type of officer that the German Panzer troops were seeking to recruit. It makes an interesting comparison with the earlier lecture of Captain Bechtolsheim:

One thing is sure – he who seeks formulae for commanding the mobile units, the pedantic type, should take off the black battledress [of the Panzer forces]. He has no idea of its spirit.

Apart from the numbers of tanks available to each side, the opposing sides (the British, French, Dutch, and Belgians on one hand, and the Germans on the other) were fairly evenly matched in terms of manpower totals and even equipment levels. It became fashionable to dismiss the Allies as outnumbered by the Germans – after all, the German population in 1940 was double that of France. But in fact, the western allies fielded 144 divisions with the Germans managing 141. Similarly, the western powers fielded 13,974 artillery pieces as against the Germans' 7,378.

In the air, the Allies again had greater numbers of aircraft, but the Germans had the advantage in terms of numbers of modern combat aircraft. They possessed the excellent Messerschimdt 109 fighter, which

The Battle of France: the race to the sea

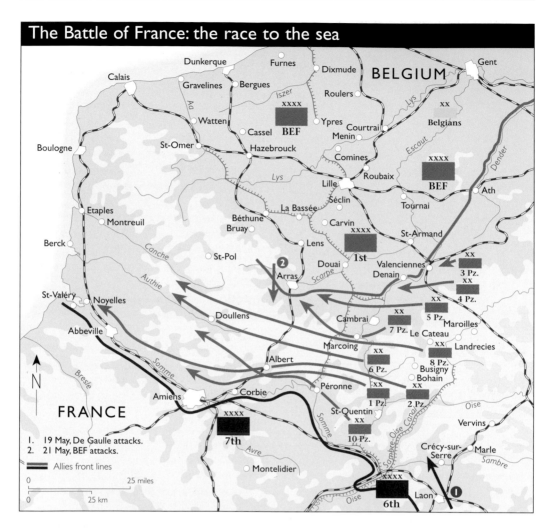

1. 19 May, De Gaulle attacks.
2. 21 May, BEF attacks.

▬ Allies front lines

0 _____ 25 miles
0 _____ 25 km

outclassed most Allied fighters. The British contribution to the air war did not include sending Spitfire aircraft to France, but only Hurricanes in limited numbers. The French Dewoitime was another good Allied aircraft, but the French air force had only around 100 machines. The Germans had used their Stuka dive-bomber to devastating effect against the Poles and the Luftwaffe possessed several hundred of these aircraft, using them in the close air-support role.

Once the lead German formations had crossed the Meuse and largely outrun their supporting infantry and logistical supplies, the western allies were presented with an opportunity to regain some of the initiative. The Germans lacked a coherent operational level plan; once they had crossed the Meuse,

they were in two minds as to where to go, either towards Paris or to take the Maginot Line from behind. Eventually the Germans decided to head for the coast and the Allies at last took their chance. The counterattack by the BEF at Arras, from the north, and the French from the south was indicative of the whole campaign. The Anglo-French forces did not operate in tandem and despite some initial success the Germans beat them off. This incident, however, did persuade Hitler to halt his leading Panzer elements and in doing so allowed the British and French vital time to organize the evacuation of their forces from Dunkirk.

Hitler, along with many senior German officers, could not quite believe how much their forces had achieved so quickly and still

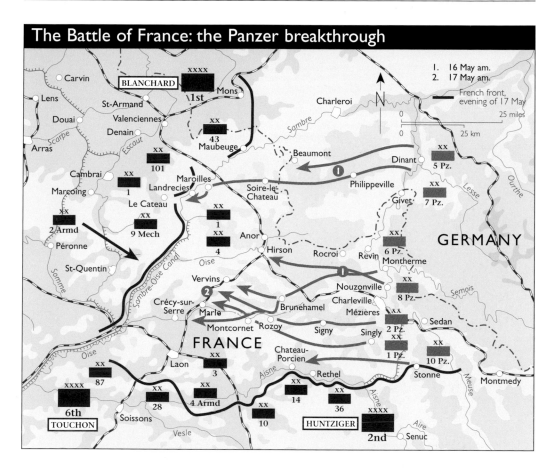

The Battle of France: the Panzer breakthrough

considered that the Allies were likely to strike back. They were wrong; Allied resistance had collapsed. After 5 June the Germans enacted *Fall Red*, the final phase of their plan to take France, occupying the rest of the country. Ironically, some elements of the Maginot Line were not defeated, but instead were ordered to give up in the general surrender of 22 June.

Operation Dynamo

Operation Dynamo began, officially, on 26 May 1940. By 4 June, 366,162 Allied troops had been successfully evacuated from the beaches around Dunkirk; of these, 53,000 were French. The price of the Dunkirk evacuations was not a light one. The RAF lost 177 aircraft over Dunkirk – losses it could ill afford – and the Royal Navy also had 10 escorts sunk. Even after the

operations around Dunkirk were over, the evacuation of Allied personnel continued from elsewhere in France, including France's Mediterranean coast, and up to the final cessation of operations on 14 August a further 191,870 were successfully rescued. In total 558,032 Allied personnel were evacuated from France between 20 May and 14 August.

Operation Dynamo has traditionally been represented, certainly in British historiography, as something of a triumph. In many respects it was so; the figures cited above are ample testimony to what was a fantastic achievement in rescuing so many Allied troops from captivity or death. A little over a month after the Dunkirk evacuation, however, three British journalists, Peter Howard of the *Sunday Express*, Frank Owen of the *Evening Standard*, and Michael Foot also of the *Standard*, wrote a devastating critique of the Dunkirk fiasco and the events that led

Queues wait for the navy at Dunkirk during Operation Dynamo, 29 May–2 June 1940. (Ann Ronan Picture Library)

up to it. This work, entitled *Guilty Men* and published with the authors' names concealed by the pseudonym 'Cato,' had a considerable impact on the general public.

Cato charged the disaster to have been caused by the prewar appeasers, men such as Ramsay MacDonald, Stanley Baldwin, and, most specifically, Neville Chamberlain himself. This notion became firmly embedded in the postwar psyche, certainly of the British. The fact that it accorded with what Winston Churchill was also to write, postwar, certainly helped this simplistic idea of appeasement to become the standard way of remembering the prewar years.

The collapse of France was to have a tragic and controversial postscript. The French Navy was large and formidable, and its inclusion in either of the warring sides would have proved significant. The British Mediterranean fleet was on a par with the Italian Navy, but the addition of the French would have tipped the delicate balance decisively. In the aftermath of the fall of French, the French fleet, under Admiral Darlan, ignored the provisions of the

Franco-German armistice, by which the French fleet was to have been disarmed under Axis supervision. Instead, a large portion of the fleet sailed to the Algerian ports of Oran and Mers el-kebir, where it had assembled by 29 June.

The British were understandably concerned about the future of the French vessels and considered a variety of options. They wished the French fleet either to join

The Ulster Rifles at Bray Dunes, 29-May–3 June 1940. (Topham Picturepoint)

Swastika over Paris. (Ann Ronan Picture Library)

with their Free French compatriots and fight
alongside the British, to sail to neutral ports,
or to scuttle their ships and thus prevent
them being utilized by the Axis powers. A
final option, described by Winston Churchill
as 'appalling,' was that the Royal Navy
would 'use whatever force was necessary' to
prevent the ships being used against Britain.
There were concerns, too, over what the
German role might be – whether or not the
Germans would apply pressure to force
Admiral Darlan to comply.

Despite last-minute talks between the
British and the French commander on the
spot, no accommodation could be reached.
The British, fearing the arrival of other
French vessels, opened fire on 3 July, killing
in the region of 1,200 French sailors. The
British officer responsible for the failed
negotiations wrote to his wife: 'It was an
absolute bloody business to shoot up those
Frenchmen ... we all feel thoroughly dirty
and ashamed.'

The Battle of Britain

In the aftermath of the rapid defeat of France
and the Low Countries, and the evacuation
of the British Expeditionary Force from

Dunkirk, few believed that Great Britain could resist Hitler for long. Indeed, the American Ambassador to the Court of St James, Joseph Kennedy – father of the future president, John F. – believed that Britain was doomed and reported the same to Washington.

In the face of the British refusal to make peace, Hitler planned an ambitious amphibious operation, codenamed Operation Sea Lion, to invade the British Isles. With the fall of France and the scrambled evacuation of Anglo-French forces from the beaches of Dunkirk, Britain stood effectively alone against Nazi Germany. On 18 June Winston Churchill told the assembled House of Commons that 'The Battle of France is over, I expect that the Battle of Britain is about to begin.'

The next logical step for Adolf Hitler was the removal of Great Britain from the strategic equation, leaving him free, in due course, to turn eastwards and accomplish his principal aim: the destruction and subjugation of the Soviet Union and the establishment of German colonies in this new *Lebensraum*. How this was to be achieved was a dilemma for Hitler, initially at least. Hitler was not an implacable opponent of the British, partly for reasons of race, and professed to admire the British Empire. What, then, of the chances for peace between Britain and Germany?

Despite some apparent British warmth for the idea of a negotiated settlement, these sentiments were fundamentally insubstantial, based as they were on the false beliefs, first, that an acceptable peace could be arrived at and, second, that suggestions of impending British acquiescence might spur both the USA from her neutrality and the Soviet Union from her collaboration with Hitler. Hitler's enunciation of his willingness to negotiate with the British was made clear in a speech on 19 July. When there was no positive response from the British, the way was clear for the planning of Operation Sea Lion – the proposed invasion of Britain by German amphibious forces.

However, any successful landing in Britain would require effective German air superiority. To achieve that, the Royal Air Force had to be

destroyed and this was to prove problematic. While the British Expeditionary Force that had been sent to France was representative of Britain's generally small army, it was the RAF and to a lesser extent the Royal Navy that had received the lion's share of defense spending in the run-up to the outbreak of war. To a large extent this money had been well spent, with new fighter aircraft such as the Hurricane being particularly effective and the even newer Spitfire setting new standards of performance for a fighter plane. The RAF had not deployed any of its Spitfire strength to France, instead holding them back for the likely air battle to follow.

The German ability to attain air superiority was hampered, in part, by the role for which the Luftwaffe had originally been conceived, that of tactical air support for troops on the ground. This focus on supporting army operations meant that in 1940 Germany lacked both a long-range bomber and a fighter with which to conduct a strategic bombing campaign. Indeed, over the course of the war Germany never rectified this position, although she did develop larger aircraft, notably the four-engine Condor, which was used for reconnaissance purposes.

The Battle of Britain has earned a significant place in British cultural as well as military history. Emboldened and honored in several trademark speeches, the 'few' of the RAF (together with a sizable Commonwealth and exile contingent of Czechs and Poles) successfully thwarted the aims of the Luftwaffe, obliging the date for Sea Lion to be progressively put off until it was finally cancelled. The Battle of Britain can conveniently be split into two distinct phases: the first from 10 July 1940 until 13 August, and the second from 13 August to 17 September, when Operation Sea Lion was postponed indefinitely. The invasion was finally cancelled on 12 October 1940.

On 19 July 1940, Hitler made a curious speech in the Reichstag. It was witnessed by American journalist William Shirer, who noted that Hitler said:

In this hour I feel it is my duty before my own conscience to appeal once more to reason and

The principal RAF and Luftwaffe bases

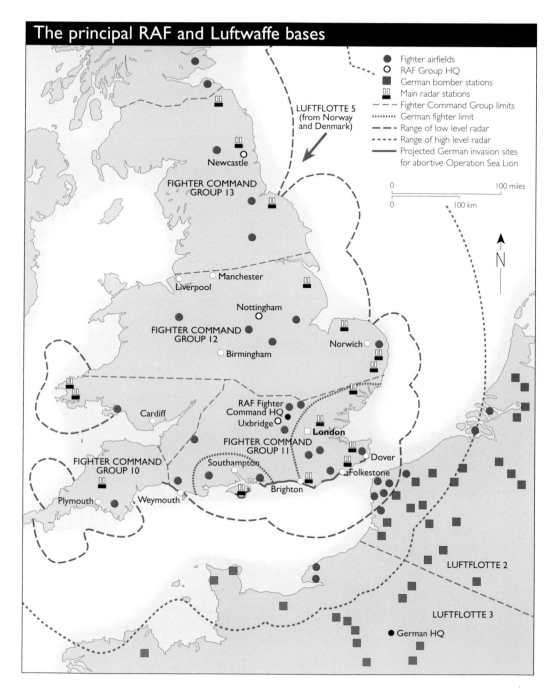

Fighter airfields
RAF Group HQ
German bomber stations
Main radar stations
Fighter Command Group limits
German fighter limit
Range of low level radar
Range of high level radar
Projected German invasion sites for abortive Operation Sea Lion

LUFTFLOTTE 5 (from Norway and Denmark)

Newcastle

FIGHTER COMMAND GROUP 13

Manchester
Liverpool

Nottingham

FIGHTER COMMAND GROUP 12

Birmingham

Norwich

RAF Fighter Command HQ
Uxbridge
London

Cardiff

FIGHTER COMMAND GROUP 11

FIGHTER COMMAND GROUP 10

Southampton

Dover

Folkestone

Plymouth   Weymouth

Brighton

LUFTFLOTTE 2

LUFTFLOTTE 3

German HQ

0   100 miles
0   100 km

N

common sense. I can see no reason why this war must go on ... I am grieved to think of the sacrifices which it will claim. I should like to avert them, also, for my own people.

Shirer admitted to wondering what the British reply to this clumsy overture for a peaceful accommodation might be. It did not take long for British feelings to be made known. Shirer heard the BBC German program announcer reply, unofficially, 'Herr Führer and Reichskanzler we hurl it right back at you, right in your evil-smelling teeth.' The official feeling was less graphically expressed but did not differ markedly.

The first phase of the German air assault was designed to secure German air superiority over the Channel – the so-called *Kanalkampf* – with the harbors of England's south coast and their associate shipping being the target. The second phase was known as the *Adlerangriff* (Eagle Attack) and began, on 13 August, with *Adlertag* (Eagle Day), which finally swept the RAF from the skies. The German bombers now concentrated on the RAF airfields themselves, destroying aircraft and pilots faster than the British could replace them,

Civilians try to sleep in a tube station during the Blitz. (Topham Picturepoint)

and threatening to overwhelm Fighter Command's ability to resist.

However, despite the odds mounting gradually in Germany's favor, a freak incident helped change the course of the battle and with it the strategic direction of the war. The accidental bombing of London by German aircraft led to a reciprocal British strike on Berlin. This prompted Hitler to his famous pronouncement, 'since they bomb our cities, we shall raze theirs to the ground,' and to the wholesale switch of German air effort toward the destruction of British cities rather than the RAF bases that defended them. On 7 September 1940, Reichsmarschal Hermann Göring told his senior Luftwaffe officers:

I now want to take this opportunity of speaking to you, to say this moment is an historic one. As a result of the provocative British attacks on Berlin on recent nights, the Führer has decided to order a mighty blow to be struck in revenge against the capital of the British Empire. I personally have assumed the leadership of this attack and today I have heard above me the roaring of the victorious German squadrons which now, for the first time, are driving towards the heart of the enemy in full daylight, accompanied by countless fighter squadrons … this is an historic hour, in which for the first time the German Luftwaffe has struck at the heart of the enemy.

This switch in tactics was a godsend for the RAF, since the breathing space allowed it to regroup and rejoin the battle. Now the battle focused on preventing German aircraft from reaching their targets over London or a score of other British targets.

While the target of German interest had changed, the ferocity of the air battles had not. Nor were losses in the air declining. During the first week of September, the RAF lost 185 aircraft and the Luftwaffe lost in excess of 200. The climax of the battle came on 15 September. Successive waves of German bombers, escorted by fighters, flew toward London and the RAF was stretched to the limit to try to contain them. The end

result was a success for Fighter Command – but only just – and a realization on the part of the Luftwaffe and Adolf Hitler that air superiority was unlikely to be achieved any time soon. 15 September, subsequently celebrated as Battle of Britain day, marked the end of German attempts to provide the right circumstances for an invasion.

The success of Fighter Command in staving off the imminent threat of German invasion did not, however, end the German bombing campaign against British cities. In fact the Blitz, as it came to be known, had only just begun. The Germans hit the Midlands city of Coventry on 14 November and followed this up with raids on Birmingham, Bristol, Manchester, and Liverpool. London, too, was obviously a massive target for the Luftwaffe as a symbol of British defiance as well as the heart of the governmental system. German bombing continued into 1941, with the last raids of the Blitz coming in May that year. German attacks on Britain resumed in the latter stages of the war as they launched initially the V1 rockets, later the V2, against London. These weapons did little real damage, but were sufficient to cause concern amongst the civilian populace.

Dieppe

Having successfully warded off the threat of imminent German invasion in 1940, the British gave considerable thought to hitting back at the Germans. One means, in the air, was the strategic bombing campaign, examined in more detail below. While the British had achieved some morale-building successes, such as the sinking of the German pocket battleship *Bismarck*, in 1942, there was widespread feeling that more should be done to strike at Hitler's 'fortress Europe.'

After the fall of France, Churchill had sanctioned the training and employment of 'commando' units to strike at targets in occupied Europe. He also created the Special Operations Executive (SOE) to 'set Europe ablaze.' The commando raids were successful in raising Allied morale and proving a nuisance to the Germans, but after successes at St Nazaire and Bruneval, the Allies determined on a more substantial foray into occupied Europe.

The aim of the Dieppe raid of August 1942 was limited in terms of what was to be achieved practically, but significant in terms of what the Allies hoped to learn about the problems involved in landing in enemy-held territory. The Allied plan, Operation Jubilee, aimed to land troops and armored vehicles on the beach and take and hold the port for 12 hours. The Allied forces, having secured the town, were to push inland and capture a German headquarters, gaining prisoners for interrogation and documents, and then to retreat back across the Channel. The Allies also hoped to cause enough damage, and to worry the Germans sufficiently, that the German High Command would withdraw forces from the Eastern Front and thereby take some pressure off the Red Army. This second aim was rather ambitious.

In the event, Dieppe was a disaster. The Allied force lost the vital ingredient of surprise when they ran into German shipping mid-Channel, and failed to secure the two headlands on either side of the main beach at Dieppe. Despite this setback, the main force landed on the beach and met considerable fire from German troops, well dug-in in blockhouses on the seafront and from the headlands. Still more Allied forces landed: 27 Churchill tanks reached the beach safely and 15 made it to the esplanade but no further.

Eventually, when it was apparent that no progress was being made, the mixture of British, Canadian, and American troops were withdrawn. This first composite Allied force, a foretaste of the Normandy landings two years hence, suffered 1,027 dead and a further 2,340 captured. However, the experience gained by the assault itself proved invaluable and prompted Admiral Lord Mountbatten to comment that 'for every soldier who died at Dieppe, ten were saved on D-Day.' While Mountbatten's comments may have proved, ultimately, to be true, he was also the man in charge of the operation.

The Battle of the Atlantic

The Battle of the Atlantic was one of the most important battles waged during the Second World War (see *The Second World War (3) The war at sea* in this series). Britain's survival, and with her the survival of the struggle against Nazi Germany, depended on feeding her population and her war machine. British industry relied on raw materials from overseas to keep functioning. These goods had to be carried to Britain across, for the most part, the Atlantic Ocean. Without the outside lifeline, Britain's ability to sustain meaningful resistance against the Axis powers would have been seriously eroded, and eventually Britain would have been starved into submission.

The means of ensuring this constant lifeline were convoys – large numbers of ships marshaled together with naval support to beat off attacks from German submarines, or U-boats. As the tactics adopted by the German submariners became ever more sophisticated, such as hunting in large Wolf Packs, and as their submarines became ever larger and more seaworthy, so too did the weapons and tactics devised by the Allies in response. These included underwater echo-finding sonar, known as asdic, depth charges, and merchant ships converted to carry aircraft launched from a catapult. The development of surface radar was also vital in enabling surface warships to detect their submarine prey on the surface, when they were at their most vulnerable. This advance allowed the surfaced U-boats to be located in darkness and helped reduce the threat from the U-boat fleet, many of whose commanders preferred to attack at night and via the surface.

Alongside the vital convoys bringing raw materials to Britain between 1939 and 1943, the British also mounted an enormous effort to send supplies to the Soviet Union in order to prop her up against the German attack, after June 1941. While the Soviet authorities consistently downplayed the amount of British (and American) aid received, it was substantial. The convoy routes from Britain to the Soviet Union, usually the northern port of Murmansk, were fraught with danger from the German U-boats and from the perilous conditions of sub-zero temperatures and mountainous seas.

The war in the Atlantic cost the lives of thousands of sailors on both sides, but by the summer of 1943 it was the Allies who were decisively in charge. The U-boats of German Admiral Dönitz's navy sank 2,600 Allied merchant vessels and over 175 naval ships; 30,000 Allied sailors also died. On the German side, out of 1,162 U-boats built, 784 were lost. Of the German crews, a staggering 26,000 sailors out of a total number of 40,000 were killed, with 5,000 men taken prisoner. The German submarine arm had come close to strangling the Allied war effort, but the cost, as a proportion of the size of the service, was unmatched.

The strategic bomber offensive

One of the most controversial elements of the Second World War was the Allied

The strategic bombing campaign

strategic bombing offensive against German-occupied Europe. The bombing of enemy cities was obviously not a new phenomenon; indeed, the Germans had carried out a limited campaign against Britain in the First World War using Zeppelin airships and Gotha aircraft. However, bombing had previously been essentially confined to a tactical role, if only because of the limitations of the fragile technology available.

Between the wars, much thought was given over to the idea of air power now being potentially a decisive weapon in war. The improvements in aeronautical engineering turned the fragile aircraft of 1914–18, with their limited range and payload capacity, into far more useful weapons. Air power theorists such as the Italian Guilo Douhet, the American William Mitchell, and the Briton Sir Hugh Dowding all prophesied that the bomber might shape the course of future

Arthur Travers Harris received the nickname 'Bomber' Harris. (Ann Ronan Picture Library)

wars. In Britain especially, the idea that the 'bomber will always get through' haunted interwar defense planners, conscious that Britain's traditional reliance on her naval strength would be inadequate. In the event this proved true, and the days of the battleship were numbered when HMS *Repulse* and HMS *Prince of Wales* were sunk by Japanese aircraft off Malaya in December 1941. However, the role of the bomber also proved to be far less decisive than the advocates of air power imagined.

On 3 September 1940, a year to the day after Britain had declared war on Germany, Winston Churchill declared that 'our supreme effort must be to gain overwhelming mastery in the air. The fighters are our salvation, but the bombers alone can provide the means to victory.' Churchill's personal commitment to the idea that the bomber could win the war was significant and had its origins in his position as the First Lord of the Admiralty when he ordered bombing raids on German Zeppelin bases. In 1917, however, Churchill's position was rather different; indeed, he considered then that 'nothing we have learned justifies us in assuming that they [German civilians] could be cowed into submission by such methods [large-scale bombing].'

On 22 February 1942, Arthur Travers Harris was appointed to the post of Chief of Royal Air Force (RAF) Bomber Command. He believed that area bombing or strategic

The Avro Lancaster bomber entered service in 1942 aand became the mainstay of the British strategic bombing campaign. (Topham Picturepoint)

bombing could win the war, and that by pounding Germany's industrial capability and destroying German cities, the will of the Germans, in tandem with the buildings around them, would collapse. This bomber offensive was no simple payback for the German raids on British cities. RAF Bomber Command pounded Germany for three years, culminating in the destruction of Dresden. The British bombers were joined in the summer of 1942 by the United States Army Air Force, whose more heavily armed B-17 'Flying Fortresses' bombed by day, and then the Allies struck around the clock in a campaign that the Germans called 'terror bombing.' Harris soon earner himself the nickname of 'Bomber' Harris amongst the general public, and 'Butch' or 'Butcher' Harris amongst his own men.

The tactics of the bombing offensive changed dramatically as the war progressed. Initial sorties were conducted by comparatively small, twin-engine aircraft such as the Vickers Wellington. The amount of ordnance that these aircraft could carry was small compared to the new, four-engine bombers that were coming into service by the time Harris took over. The introduction of the Short Stirling and later the Avro Lancaster revolutionized the distance that the bomber raids could fly, and thus the range of targets that could be hit, as well as increasing exponentially the bomb tonnage that could be carried.

A confidential report, prepared in 1941, highlighted some of the worrying problems associated with the bombing campaign and undermined the claims by the bomber

advocates that they were capable of winning the war on their own. The report, gleaned from aerial photographs of bomb targets, concluded that only one aircraft in three was able to get within 5 miles (8km) of its allocated target and that their accuracy was often even less impressive. The overall percentage of aircraft that managed to arrive within 75 square miles (194km^2) of the target was as low as 20 percent.

The net result of these inaccuracies was the creation and adoption of a new tactic, that of 'area bombing.' This eschewed the attempted precision raids of the past in favor of the destruction not only of factories but also of their hinterland: the surrounding towns, complete with the workers who lived there. This policy, unfairly attributed to Harris himself, was the product of a decision not to adopt terror tactics, but rather to ameliorate the shortcomings inherent in bombing so inaccurately. It was also hoped that the net effect of this type of destruction, to civilians, would result in the gradual erosion of morale amongst the civilian population. Potentially, it might either bring about the collapse of the will to resist or, more ambitiously, and more unlikely, induce a war-weary population to overthrow Adolf Hitler's administration.

The German response to the Allied bombing offensive was an impressive defensive arrangement that also grew in sophistication, in tandem with the bomber formations that it was conceived to thwart, as technological advances combined with tactical reappraisals. Luftwaffe General Josef Kammhuber was appointed to lead the air defense provision for the Reich and initially achieved some startling successes. He devised a grid system, with each square in the grid being 20 square miles (52km^2), and located a fighter in each square – held there by air traffic control and guided by radar to its target whenever a bomber or bomber formation entered its airspace.

British bomber tactics had initially focused on sending aircraft into occupied Europe singly, at intervals, and Kammhuber's approach was ideally suited to dealing with them. Later, however, with larger numbers of aircraft available, the British simply swamped the German defensive arrangements. In fact, much of the strategic value of the bombing campaign lay in the extent to which it diverted valuable resources of men and equipment away from vital front-line areas. The intensity of the bombing obliged the Germans to relocate artillery pieces as flak guns in Germany, rather than deploying them against the Soviets on the Eastern Front.

While concentrations of bombers, bringing all their firepower together, had improved their survivability in the skies over Germany, a second Allied initiative would help turn the course of the bomber offensive in a decisive fashion. This development was the introduction of fighter escorts for the whole duration of the bombing mission. It was made possible by the adoption of long-range fuel tanks, a practice that was very common when deploying fighters over long distances, but which had failed to be considered practical for combat purposes. The introduction of the Anglo-American P51 Mustang brought immediate results.

The strategic bombing campaign has been the cause of much controversy since the end of the Second World War. Elements of it, in particular Operation Gomorra (the firestorm raids on Hamburg) and the destruction of the baroque city of Dresden, are cited as evidence of how far democracies, too, are forced to go in a 'total war.' Alongside the many charges of wanton slaughter of civilians leveled at Bomber Command and its chief, Arthur Harris, are also less inflammatory ones. These allegations are more practical and center on the claim that, particularly in the early years of the war, the strategic bomber offensive was a criminal waste of men and materials that would have been better employed elsewhere. It has been argued that the overall impact on Germany's war-fighting ability was far less than it should have been, given the resources expended. However, as Richard Overy comments:

There has always seemed something fundamentally implausible about the contention of bombing's critics that dropping almost 2.5 million tons of bombs on tautly-stretched industrial systems and war-weary urban populations would not seriously weaken them. Germany ... had no special immunity.

Donald Edgar

In 1940 Donald Edgar joined the reserve element of the British army, the Territorial Army. As a barely trained private soldier in the East Surrey Regiment, he was sent to France along with rest of the British Expeditionary Force in much the same fashion as the original BEF had gone in 1914. Unlike the BEF of 20 or so years previously, however, the BEF of 1940 was not to halt the German advance. Edgar himself was captured by the Germans and spent the next five years as a prisoner of war of the Germans.

Donald Edgar, along with many thousands of young men, responded to a government appeal in March 1939 to join the Territorial Army. Adolf Hitler had occupied Czechoslovakia and it was apparent to many that the war was highly likely, if not inevitable. Edgar was in many ways an atypical private soldier, having attended Dulwich School, where he served with the Officer Training Corps, and Oxford University, from where he went to work as a stockbroker in the City of London. Edgar wrote of his enlistment that 'I was patriotic and there was a general feeling around in the City ... that it was time for us young men "to do something."' Edgar was also keen to volunteer, rather than await what he considered to be the inevitable conscription, declaring that 'No one in my family had ever been conscripted. They had always been volunteers.'

Edgar's unit was part of the British 12th Division, one of three 'second-line'

British troops pose in a well-construced position in the winter of 1939–40 in France. (IWM)

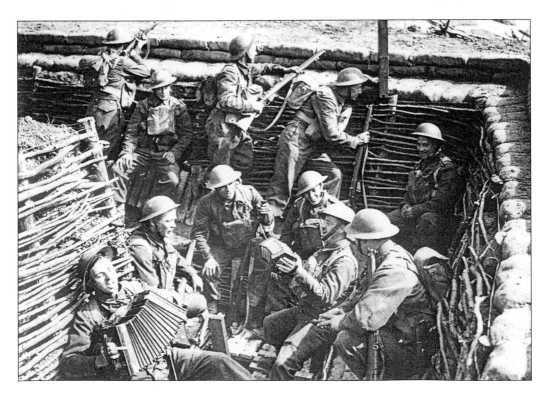

formations that Edgar considered to have been 'denied equipment and arms' and left to perform 'humdrum, menial tasks that left no time for training.' Edgar believed that the War Office thought these units were little more than a 'bloody nuisance.' This was an especial injustice for Donald Edgar and one that he felt all the more keenly because, as he put it, 'the ranks of these battalions contained a large proportion of the men who had patriotically responded to the Government's call in the spring. They were the real volunteers of the war.'

Edgar was called up in August 1939 and reported to his unit at the Richmond Drill Hall. He was fortunate to be made a number of financial guarantees by his employers in the City and he noted also that they gave him a 'handsome gift' to help him on his way, following a 'glass or two of champagne' at his farewell luncheon. This rather pleasant farewell was followed by a rude introduction to the realities of army life.

Edgar's unit moved to a camp near Chatham, a naval dockyard on the south coast of England, where they were each issued with five rounds of live ammunition and told, 'This is real guard duty, see?' Edgar's experiences of the regular British army were not positive: the conditions of their initial camp and the reception granted him by two regular warrant officers were described as 'lazy inefficiency' and 'only the first example we were to experience of the Regular Army's appalling state of slackness.'

At 11.15 am on 3 September, Edgar and his comrades listened to Prime Minister Neville Chamberlain's speech announcing Britain's declaration of war on Germany. On this momentous occasion, according to Edgar, Chamberlain gave his speech 'as though he were giving one of his budget talks on the radio when he were Chancellor.'

After a month or so at Chatham, Edgar's unit moved back to Richmond, where they were employed guarding 'vulnerable points' – the railway bridge over the Thames being Edgar's own duty. He recalled the mood that seemed to pervade the country during the 'phony war,' a mood that seemed to suggest

that Britain was doing all it could to honor her promise to Poland – even though that country had already been dismembered by Germany and the Soviet Union. Edgar thought the British had 'convinced ourselves that by mobilising the fleet and sending a few divisions to France we had done just about all that was necessary for the war against Germany.'

Despite Edgar's many complaints about the wider conduct of Britain's war effort, he himself was successively promoted through lance-corporal, corporal, and lance-sergeant, working in the unit's Intelligence Section. Edgar's unit spent a long and cold winter in England, relocating to Richmond Park and undergoing occasional training forays in the wide expanse of parkland on offer.

In March 1940, Edgar's unit was told that they were to proceed to France where they would at last 'train hard and receive all our equipment from supplies already there.' They embarked for France and landed at Le Havre, before moving to a large château in the Normandy countryside. Edgar's bilingual capability led to his being appointed as a translator and he participated in a number of meetings between his battalion commander and the local French military authorities. These meetings Edgar termed 'predictably uncomfortable,' but 'no more so than those held at the highest level between French and British generals.' Given the lack of adequate coordination between the French and British forces in France, it is interesting to see these considerations replicated at the battalion level.

Because of his evident language capabilities, Edgar was tasked with translating a number of documents that the French had passed on to their British counterparts. These documents concerned the French arrangements to defend the important dock areas of Le Havre, but they had wider implications for the forthcoming fighting – implications and conclusions that had Edgar concerned: 'When I came to translate the French documents I was shaken out of my complacency. The analysis envisaged a war of movement as a distinct possibility with the breakthrough of German armoured columns deep into the rear areas.' These conclusions, as we have seen, were to prove extremely accurate. As Edgar also noted, however, the officers now leading his and many other battalions of the British and French armies had seen service on the Western Front during 1914–18 and this was not the type of war they were accustomed to.

Donald Edgar obviously had many criticisms of the British army. Many of these may be dismissed as the typical grumbling of any soldier; some are more valid, however. Edgar informs us that many units were short of machine guns and antitank weapons, what they did possess being far less than the official complement. What Edgar considered to be the worst omission was one of the areas in which the Germans had both a marked superiority and, perhaps even more crucially, a greater understanding of its importance: communications. While Edgar conceded that the regular BEF units were provided with wireless and telephone communications, the men of the three 'labour' battalions had neither and 'went forward blind.' This was an unsatisfactory state of affairs at any time, but given the manner in which the Germans utilized new technology in combination with rather less original tactics, these shortcomings were particularly damaging to the effective conduct of the war on the Allied side.

Despite all the problems identified by Donald Edgar, writing on the eve of battle, he was not totally pessimistic about the future. Edgar believed that 'the spirit of the men was still high – in spite of everything.' Although Edgar's reminiscences at this point perhaps border on the sentimental, he comments that 'it is with a bitter smile that those English Territorial battalions [went] to battle in May 1940 with a raucous laugh, singing a silly song: "Roll out the barrel."'

Edgar's experiences of the fighting are interesting. He noted that his:

Intelligence section travelled in three handy 15 cwt trucks and were just about self contained. We had ample ammunition for our rifles and

brens and reserve supplies of petrol … I made sure … that we had plenty of cigarettes and bottles of whisky and brandy.

Edgar thought that these preparations were:

to prove vital in the following days. It gave us a certain confidence, and an army marches – even in trucks – on its stomach. A swig or two of spirits and a cigarette also help to keep up morale. Other units in the area were reduced to begging for food and water.

While Edgar's unit waited for further orders he noticed a 'tall figure in khaki standing on some rising ground … wearing one of those beautifully-tailored near ankle length great-coats favoured by senior officers. I looked again and saw the red tabs and realized he was probably a Brigadier or General.' Edgar was shocked to see that the officer was 'unshaven and bore marks of dishevelment,' which Edgar considered unforgivable, observing: 'I am shaved. So are my men. That's discipline … Generals should never appear unshaven or unkempt. They must always be immaculately turned-out. It is part of an army's morale!'

In all probability, however, it would have taken more than morale alone to save the British (and indeed French) position in France in May 1940. While awaiting further instructions, Edgar ran into a column of refugees who included in their number a former British soldier of the 1914–18 war. This man, now in his forties, had met a French girl during that war and returned after leaving the army to marry her and set up a business renting holiday cottages. The man quizzed Edgar about the development of the fighting and after Edgar informed him that he expected the French to counterattack, the former British soldier, Edgar observed, 'sniffed disbelievingly.'

The evident disbelief was to prove reasonably well founded, as the counterattacks that were planned, notably the initially successful BEF attack at Arras, soon ran out of steam. Edgar found himself and his men surrounded by the fast-moving German forces. After retreating toward the small French port of Veules, Edgar was given instructions to take a message to his battalion commanding officer at St Valery. When he made the obvious point that 'it won't be easy, Sir, the French tell me that the Germans have cut just about all the roads,' Edgar was told that 'this message must get through.' Edgar and two other men set off, and while they were gone, the officer who had ordered Edgar to St Valery evacuated the rest of the unit.

Edgar managed to rejoin his unit and with men from other units began the march towards the sea. Reaching St Valery, they were told that 'evacuation was now impossible' due to the deteriorating situation, and tentative plans were made to attempt to break through the German lines in small groups. These plans, too, came to nothing with the announcement on 12 June of a cease-fire. Edgar and some 8,000 BEF soldiers went into captivity. Edgar himself survived five years in a German prisoner-of-war camp, but had not fired a single shot in anger during the whole duration of the battle for France.

The home front

While the war was felt most keenly by those engaged in its prosecution – the military at the sharp end of the conflict – the war impacted on the wider world in a host of other ways. Indeed, as the war progressed, virtually the whole society of the respective participants became involved and the distinction between combatant and non-combatant become less clear: the munitions worker was arguably as central to the successful conduct of the war as the soldier who used their product. Many of the changes wrought by the war years would not dissipate with the end of the fighting, but would remain part of the permanent fabric of society. In this respect, as well as in the political/military sphere, the war's impact was enormous.

Great Britain

On the home front, in Britain at least, the war changed every facet of daily life. The British government had begun the transition to a war economy – an economy that was planned and directed with the specific aim of furthering the prosecution of the war – only with the outbreak of hostilities in September 1939. Thereafter, the extent of mobilization, economic, military, social, and political, of all of Britain's national resources was astonishing. By 1945 Britain had mobilized and utilized all her latent potential to a far greater extent than any other of the major belligerents.

This degree of government control and the success achieved by state direction translated directly into the massive electoral landslide achieved by Clement Attlee's Labour Party in the 1945 general election. Millions of Britons had become convinced between 1939 and 1945 that the government could direct the economy and do so successfully. The apparent demonstration of government effectiveness in fighting and winning a war was seen as a recipe for the postwar government doing similarly for national prosperity, to provide the 'land fit for heroes' that had proved so elusive post-1918.

In 1942 William Beveridge published his report on the shape of postwar Britain. It aimed to defeat the 'Five Giants on the Road to Recovery': these were Want, Disease, Ignorance, Squalor and Idleness. To achieve this, Beveridge planned a comprehensive welfare system, which was to become, in effect, the welfare state. Much effort was made to publicize the report and its findings, and within a month of its publication over 100,000 copies had been sold – an astonishing feat for a government paper. By 1943, the Gallup polling organization reported that 19 out of 20 people had heard of the report. The people of Britain, then, knew exactly what they were fighting for in terms of a new Britain.

The means to implement Beveridge was, of course, far greater government control of all aspects of life, as demonstrated by the successful utilization of national resources during wartime. What then, did this state control amount to? A large proportion of the devolved responsibility for economic production fell on women, due to the service of the men in the armed services. Some 80,000 women served in the Land Army, working as agricultural laborers and ensuring that every available acre of Britain's farmland was under cultivation. Similarly, those with private gardens or allotments were urged to 'dig for victory' to increase the level of food production.

The British population contributed in other ways to the war effort. Every available piece of metal was hoarded and used – not only scrap, but decorative iron railings were ripped up to aid the construction of ships and tanks. The effects of these levels of mobilization on production levels were significant: for example, tank production rose from 969 in 1939 to 8,611 in 1942. Drives to secure spare aluminum pots and pans to be used in the construction of aircraft were accompanied by such catchy phrases as 'Stop 'em frying, keep 'em flying.' This kind of advertising, buoyed, of course, by the widespread realization of what such sacrifices meant, was remarkably successful. The spirit of selflessness and self-sacrifice appeared to be a national one: for instance, crime in Britain fell from 787,000 convictions for all crimes in 1939 to 467,000 in 1945.

One of the most traumatic elements of the conflict, for the civilians of the UK, was not the bombing or even the knowledge of the dangers being faced by loved ones

RAF recruiting station. (Topham Picturepoint)

involved in the fighting, but simply the policy of evacuation. The evacuation of large numbers of children away from urban areas was controversial and produced many unhappy parents, children, and host families, as children were sent far away from their homes and established routines, to remote parts of the British Isles. For many, it was the Empire that was their destination, with some being evacuated as far away as Canada and Australia, and many failing to return at the cessation of hostilities in 1945.

The USA

While Britain mobilized to the greatest extent in relative terms, it was, predictably, the United States that mobilized the most in absolute terms. Approximately 16 million Americans served in the armed forces and around 10 million American women stepped into the jobs that they had vacated. The wholesale switch of the vast potential of the American economy from peacetime, civil

American women working in industry.
(AKG Berlin)

production to war materials is perhaps best illustrated by a few bald statistics. In 1941 the American automobile industry, and the three main manufacturers, Ford, General Motors, and Chrysler, together produced in excess of 3 ½ million vehicles – a record for the auto-industry. The next year, the first complete one of American participation in the war, saw this level of car production fall to just 139 vehicles. The whole productive capacity had been refocused on war production. It was this vast economic power that the Axis powers now had to face.

The influx of large numbers of American service personnel into Britain also had a big impact. The American forces, although obviously contributing in a profound fashion to the Allied war effort, were not always accepted so readily on a local level. The

Propoganda poster showing Churchilll. (Topham Picturepoint)

epithet 'over-paid, over-sexed, and over here' was thought by many Britons to be wholly appropriate. The exodus of in excess of 50,000 GI brides at the end of the war suggests, perhaps, that they were at least partly right.

Germany

The war changed everyday life in Germany just as it did in the rest of Europe. But it did not come home to the German people as forcibly and as quickly as it did to the rest of the major combatants. One reason is that, while the British and Americans made maximum use of female labor, in jobs and

By 3 September 1,500,000 had been evacuated from urban areas. Later many left for Canada and Australia, some never to return. (Topham Picturepoint)

WOMEN OF BRITAIN
COME INTO
THE FACTORIES

Women of Britain poster. (Topham Picturepoint

industries traditionally monopolized by men, Germany was comparatively late in doing so. Nazi ideology stressed the role of the woman as a mother and homemaker. The need for women to occupy jobs in the workplace was not easily reconciled with this traditional perspective of women's role in society.

Such considerations contributed to the tardiness with which the German economy adapted to the demands of a total war. Hitler's initial successes in Europe were predicated above all on short campaigns and therefore did not require a more galvanized economy to support the military effort. Not until 1943 did the German economy begin to respond in a more concerted fashion to the demands of total war. On 18 February the first official decrees about what was needed were announced by the Nazi propaganda minister, Josef Goebbels. All men between the ages of 16 and 65 were to be registered and available to work for the state. Also at this time an estimated

100,000 women were called up to staff anti-aircraft batteries and handle searchlights. While these initiatives and figures may seem impressive, they were later and far lower than, in particular, the British.

While the Germans may have been comparatively slow in adapting the economy to the demands of a total war, they responded to the outbreak of war in much the same fashion as the other combatants. Blackouts in urban areas, petrol rationing, and food rationing had all been introduced by the end of September 1939. The weekly meat ration for German civilians was fixed at 1lb (450g) per person. Clothes rationing was also introduced with points being allocated per person per year: 150 points represented the average allowance; a pair of women's stockings would account for 4 points, while 60 points would purchase a man's suit.

These restrictions were not particularly pleasant, but equally they were not unbearable. Indeed, as many testified, the generations of Germans that had lived through the lean years of the 1920s and 1930s did not find such shortages particularly onerous. However, of course, worse was to come – much worse. The war began to bite deeply in the winter of 1941–42 when the lack of farmers to harvest crops, especially the unrationed potatoes,

Propoganda posters were used by both sides during this war. This image shows the line up of nations united against Hitler. (Topham Picturepoint)

your **BRITAIN** · *fight for it now*

ISSUED BY A.B.C.A.

This British propaganda poster shows an idyllic country view. (Topham Picturepoint)

really began to be felt. In June 1941 the bread and meat rations were reduced; nearly a year later the fats allowances were also reduced and the ubiquitous potatoes were finally included on the ration scale.

German civilians endured the effects of ever-decreasing rations and, in the latter stages of the war, almost round-the-clock bombing from the RAF by night and the USAAF by day. Underpinning it all was a constant nagging doubt, reinforced by the growing numbers of refugees and wounded servicemen, that the war could not really be won. These feelings obviously grew considerably after the fall of Stalingrad in January 1943. From then on, many German civilians began to doubt the inevitability of the final victory, although the persistent attention of the state security apparatus, and the swift and brutal response to dissent, ensured that few were either brave or foolish enough to voice their suspicions.

There hung a darker shadow over Germany during this time – the Holocaust.

The treatment of German Jews had worsened progressively. The early days of Nazi rule saw uncoordinated and localized abuse of Germany's Jewish population. The enactment of the 'Nuremberg Laws,' which effectively stripped Jews of any rights in Nazi Germany, was merely the beginning of something much worse. As the German war machine moved eastwards, overrunning territory and population, it also encountered millions of Polish and Russian Jews. Some were shot in mass killings and many others were corralled into walled areas of major cities, known as ghettos. The Jewish 'problem' was, for the Nazis, becoming intractable.

In early 1942 a selection of key officials under Heydrich, including men such as Adolf Eichmann and 'Gestapo' Muller, met at a villa in Wannsee, south of Berlin. Here they decided on the 'final solution' to the 'Jewish problem': the large-scale gassing of the Jews in places such as Auschwitz, Treblinka, Dachau, Belsen, and Buchenwald. Although the final number of Jews and other 'undesirables,' such as homosexuals, gypsies, and disabled people, killed by the Nazis is unknown, it is probably in the region of six million.

Poland

For the inhabitants of occupied Europe, the war itself was over and they faced life under German occupation. For many, this would prove even worse than the fighting. It was the Poles who suffered most, under the Germans in the western portion of their country and the Soviets in the east. As a result of the invasion by the Germans and the Soviets, Poland ceased to exist as an independent nation-state. The country was split into a number of separate pieces. The German portion was split into two, as that area of territory lost by Germany at Versailles was restored to the borders of the Reich, while the remaining area became termed the 'General Government.'

The Polish campaign had been blighted by numerous acts of cruelty by German formations – SS and police units mainly – and these incidents had been the subject of frequent, largely ineffectual protests by officers in the German army proper. Now, with Poland defeated, those isolated acts of cruelty were approved in the highest quarters of Nazi Germany and were formalized into a program of terror. In the quasi-scientific racial hierarchy that underpinned Nazi ideology, the Poles were considered sub-humans, *Untermenschen*. They suffered accordingly. During the years of the German occupation, six million Polish citizens died. Poland, alone of the occupied countries of Europe, had no collaboration with the German authorities to speak of.

France

France was rather a different proposition from Poland. Although the French were not considered the racial equals of the Aryan Germans, nor were they considered akin to the Slavs. Initially at least, France did not fare too badly after the surrender to Germany. During the interwar years there had been many elements of French society who approved of Hitler and applauded the type of right-wing authoritarianism that he

had introduced, apparently so successfully, in Germany. The roots of this apparently illogical support lay not in a particular love of Germany but rather in the fear that many felt for the power of the left, of communism and all it stood for. Just as Anglo-French concern to balance the Soviet Union with a strong Germany had inadvertently aided the rise of Hitler and his consolidation of power, so too did it provide an element of indifference toward what was to come.

There were other considerations, too, that underlay the French response to the surrender. It is hard to escape the conclusion that the substance of French resistance to the German attack of May 1940 was very different from that of 1914 and most certainly from that of 1916, when the Germans had tried, in vain, to 'bleed the French army white' at Verdun. In 1940 the will to resist was not as strong as in the Great War, and the Great War was the reason for it. The French people had seen their country devastated and her population slaughtered between 1914 and 1918. May 1940 was the third German invasion in 70 years. This goes some way toward explaining the way in which many, if by no means all, Frenchmen responded to defeat.

France was divided physically and spiritually. On one side of this division were those who wished to carry on fighting the Germans. These Frenchmen had as their figurehead General Charles de Gaulle, appointed Under-Secretary for Defense on 10 June. He left France for London, determined to carry on the fight until France was free. His views were echoed by many left behind in France, who resolved to form resistance groups and to harry the Germans in any way possible.

Others in France did not feel the same way. This element was exemplified by Marshal Pétain, the hero of the French army and nation, and the defender of Verdun in the First World War. Pétain, the Deputy Prime Minister, who had increasingly encouraged Paul Reynaud, the Prime Minister, to seek an armistice with the Germans, was asked (by President Lebrun) on 16 June to form a ministry and to arrange a cessation of hostilities. On 22 June 1940, French delegates signed the armistice that brought an end to the German campaign in France. The treaty was stage managed by Hitler personally, with the armistice signed in the same railway carriage at Compiègne that had been used for the armistice in November 1918. Hitler had exacted the revenge on France that he had long desired.

Just as Germany had been dismembered and humiliated in 1918, so too was France in 1940. While Pétain and his government were to remain nominally in power, their country was divided in two. The northern part of France, the Atlantic coast, and the border areas with Belgium and Switzerland were to be occupied by the Germans. In the south, Pétain and his government would retain control, holding their capital at the provincial town of Vichy.

Pétain changed the national motto of France from *liberté, egalité, fraternité* (freedom, equality and brotherhood) to the more national socialist sounding *travail, famille, patrie* (work, family, country). With the initial emphasis on work, it has uncomfortable echoes of *Arbeit macht frei* (work will liberate you) that was inscribed on the main gates of the Auschwitz concentration camp. While Vichy France was to retain control over France's colonial territories, all French servicemen captured by the Germans were to remain as prisoners of war, and this included the large garrison of the defunct Maginot Line, even though these men had never surrendered.

Vichy France was unique amongst all the conquered territories of the Third Reich in being the only legitimate and legally constituted government that collaborated openly with the German invaders. The whole existence of the Vichy regime, and the widespread popular support that it commanded, has been a source of tremendous embarrassment for France, post-1945. As well as acquiescing in the German takeover, the Vichy government was also anti-Semitic in outlook and responsible for the identification and subsequent deportation of many French Jews.

In November 1942 the Germans moved to end the bizarre division of France and occupied the southern portion of the country. The simultaneous invasion of French North Africa, Operation Torch, by combined Anglo-American forces allowed many Frenchmen to make another choice over their allegiances in the war. While the Anglo-French occupation of North Africa was resisted by the French Imperial troops stationed there initially, French forces eventually came around and joined the Allied cause, helped by the obvious change in circumstances of Pétain's government in France, now effectively a prisoner of the Germans. Despite the limited support that de Gaulle's Free French forces had enjoyed since 1940, the formation of the Committee of National Liberation in June 1943 gave France a government-in-exile, free from foreign direction.

Resistance

While the Vichy regime commanded considerable support, for a variety of reasons, not all Frenchmen were happy with the situation, especially those in the north, under German occupation after the surrender. Indeed, resistance movements sprang up all over occupied France and all over occupied Europe in general. Resistance fighters came from all walks of life: sometimes they were ex-soldiers, many were civilians, and many were women.

The Allies attempted to support the burgeoning resistance movement in occupied Europe. Organizations such as the British Special Operations Executive (SOE) and later the American Office of Strategic Services (OSS) were established to provide material support, such as weapons and explosives, which were parachuted in. They also supplied agents who could help coordinate resistance activities and provide skilled wireless operators to maintain contacts with London.

The French surrender at Compiegne , 21 June 1940.
They are agreeing terms in the same railway carriage in
which the Germans had signed the 1918 Armistice.
(AKG Berlin)

The life of resistance fighters was fraught
with danger, especially in the early years,
with many being betrayed to the Germans
and either imprisoned or shot out of hand.
Although the true number of those killed
will probably never be known for certain,
it is estimated that in the region of
150,000 Frenchmen and women were killed
during the German occupation and many
more in other countries.

One of the most successful and audacious
acts of resistance involved the assassination of
the Governor of the Czech portion of
Czechoslovakia, Reinhard Heydrich. This act
would demonstrate the full potential of
resistance as well as all the dangers. Heydrich,
then serving as the Deputy Protector of
Bohemia-Moravia, and also Himmler's deputy
as leader of the Gestapo security apparatus,
was killed by British-trained and equipped
Czech patriots, parachuted into their
homeland with the specific aim of killing
him. However, the operation did not go
according to plan. The SOE men initially tried
to shoot Heydrich, but the Sten gun jammed

at the vital moment and another man instead
threw a hand-grenade. This grenade failed to
kill Heydrich on the spot, but he later
succumbed to blood poisoning – the result of
the horsehair stuffing of his car seats entering
his system after the bomb thrown by the
would-be assassin exploded.

The German response to the attack was
swift and brutal. The two principal assassins,
Jan Kubis and Josef Bagcik, were hunted down
and eventually trapped in a church in Prague,
where, surrounded by German troops and
police, they killed themselves rather than
surrender. Their fate, at least, was quick. The
German reprisals were less so. In response, an
SS police unit surrounded and destroyed the
Czech village of Liddice. The village was burnt
to the ground; all the male inhabitants were
shot with the women and children being sent
to Ravensbruck concentration camp. Nine
children were spared as they were considered
to be racially suitable for adoption.

This massacre was followed by a general
clampdown on resistance activity. In total
probably 5,000 people were killed as direct
retribution for the assassination of Heydrich –
a terrible figure and one that would cause
subsequent missions to be reconsidered
in light of the probable response of the
German occupiers.

Evening Press

No. 10,972   REGISTERED AT THE G.P.O.   POSTAGE 1d.   GUERNSEY, MONDAY, JULY 1, 1940   TELEPHONE 1500 (FIVE LINES)   GRATIS
AS A NEWSPAPER.

ORDERS OF THE COMMANDANT OF THE GERMAN FORCES IN OCCUPATION OF THE ISLAND OF GUERNSEY

(1)—ALL INHABITANTS MUST BE INDOORS BY 11 P.M. AND MUST NOT LEAVE THEIR HOMES BEFORE 6 A.M.

(2)—WE WILL RESPECT THE POPULATION IN GUERNSEY; BUT, SHOULD ANYONE ATTEMPT TO CAUSE THE LEAST TROUBLE, SERIOUS MEASURES WILL BE TAKEN AND THE TOWN WILL BE BOMBED.

(3)—ALL ORDERS GIVEN BY THE MILITARY AUTHORITY ARE TO BE STRICTLY OBEYED.

(4)—ALL SPIRITS MUST BE LOCKED UP IMMEDIATELY, AND NO SPIRITS MAY BE SUPPLIED, OBTAINED OR CONSUMED HENCEFORTH. THIS PROHIBITION DOES NOT APPLY TO STOCKS IN PRIVATE HOUSES.

(5)—NO PERSON SHALL ENTER THE AERODROME AT LA VILLIAZE.

(6)—ALL RIFLES, AIRGUNS, PISTOLS, REVOLVERS, DAGGERS, SPORTING GUNS, AND ALL OTHER WEAPONS WHATSOEVER, EXCEPT SOUVENIRS, MUST, TOGETHER WITH ALL AMMUNITION, BE DELIVERED AT THE ROYAL HOTEL BY 12 NOON TO-DAY, JULY 1.

(7)—ALL BRITISH SAILORS, AIRMEN AND SOLDIERS ON LEAVE IN THIS ISLAND MUST REPORT AT THE POLICE STATION AT 9 A.M. TO-DAY, AND MUST THEN REPORT AT THE ROYAL HOTEL.

(8)—NO BOAT OR VESSEL OF ANY DESCRIPTION, INCLUDING ANY FISHING BOAT, SHALL LEAVE THE HARBOURS OR ANY OTHER PLACE WHERE THE SAME IS MOORED, WITHOUT AN ORDER FROM THE MILITARY AUTHORITY, TO BE OBTAINED AT THE ROYAL HOTEL. ALL BOATS ARRIVING FROM JERSEY, FROM SARK OR FROM HERM, OR ELSEWHERE, MUST REMAIN IN HARBOUR UNTIL PERMITTED BY THE MILITARY TO LEAVE.

THE CREWS WILL REMAIN ON BOARD. THE MASTER WILL REPORT TO THE HARBOURMASTER, ST. PETER-PORT, AND WILL OBEY HIS INSTRUCTIONS.

(9)—THE SALE OF MOTOR SPIRIT IS PROHIBITED, EXCEPT FOR USE ON ESSENTIAL SERVICES, SUCH AS DOCTORS' VEHICLES, THE DELIVERY OF FOODSTUFFS, AND SANITARY SERVICES WHERE SUCH VEHICLES ARE IN POSSESSION OF A PERMIT FROM THE MILITARY AUTHORITY TO OBTAIN SUPPLIES.

THESE VEHICLES MUST BE BROUGHT TO THE ROYAL HOTEL BY 12 NOON TO-DAY TO RECEIVE THE NECESSARY PERMISSION.

THE USE OF CARS FOR PRIVATE PURPOSES IS FORBIDDEN.

(10)—THE BLACK-OUT REGULATIONS ALREADY IN FORCE MUST BE OBSERVED AS BEFORE.

German instructions for Guernsey. Jersey and Guernsey
were liberated on 9 May 1945, Alderney not until 16 May.

Colin Perry

Colin Perry was just 18 years old when war broke out in September 1939. He lived in the London suburb of Tooting and worked as a clerk in the City of London. He kept a journal of his thoughts and experiences from June 1940, just after the fall of France, until November 1940. These few months were crucial for Britain, and therefore for the whole remaining effort to thwart Nazi Germany's goals. Britain stood alone during this period and endured the constant threat of invasion and aerial bombardment. Colin Perry's account of life during these dark months is fascinating, as it reflects the hopes and fears of a young man who cannot help seeing the war as much as an adventure as something to be feared.

Once the news of France's capitulation was known, young Colin Perry's account was full of contradictory ideas and thoughts. He said 'condemn him to hell who is responsible for bringing Britain to the verge of existence – Britain whom we love and whom our ancestors placed into the leadership of the world.' Colin considered, from a viewpoint of considerable personal disappointment, that 'Red tape is our course. Maybe I'm embittered at having passed the Medical A1, just because I do not possess a school certificate I cannot get into the flying part of the RAF.' He was also a young man with considerable imagination. While listing all the young women to whom he had been attracted in the past, he noted that one, a German girl with whom he had spent 'a day and a half' in London in 1938, was 'charming and extraordinarily attractive but I suspect her of 5th column work'!

On 17 July, Colin reported the following dramatic developments:

Tonight in our proud Island prepare ourselves for the word that the invader has commenced his attack. The air raid wardens have passed information round that the Military at Tolworth will tonight throw up a smoke-screen, which will spread and envelop the whole metropolis, blot out vital objectives and generally throw invading hordes into confusion.

His dramatic smokescreen did not materialize and instead he paid a visit to the cinema, where he saw the propaganda film, *Britain at Bay*. The impact of this on Colin was dramatic. He claimed it 'made me want to join the army tomorrow' – doubtless the intention of the production.

Colin, for all his focus on the war and the preparations for the imminent invasion, betrays the preoccupations of teenagers the world over in his writing. Interspersed with his comments about joining up are many about girls, particularly one whom he saw on a regular basis, but whom he had not as yet summoned up the courage to ask out. Colin, who could imagine himself fighting the enemy, could not similarly conceive of this girl taking him seriously.

On 19 July the RAF, hard pressed at this point in the Battle of Britain, contacted Colin to inform him, in a 'circular,' that they would be postponing any application of his for aircrew for at least a month. Colin's response to this was that 'I do want to get in the Services before the winter, as I shall then save myself the price of a new overcoat, hat etc.' While visiting a friend's flat near Chancery Lane, Colin thought that the many barrage balloons rising above the city looked very much like so many 'soft, flabby, silvery floating elephants.'

On 30 July, Colin experienced his first raid when a solitary German aircraft dropped bombs on Esher, killing and wounding five people. The searchlights in the vicinity of Colin's house were used only briefly, in the hope of persuading the pilot that he was in fact over a rural area rather than the fringes of London itself.

As July became August, Colin became increasingly convinced that the long-predicted German invasion was likely to come sooner rather than later. On 9 August he was writing that 'the invasion did not come yesterday. Now people think Hitler will try today or tomorrow, both dates of which are favourable to his star. I maintain he will strike on 22nd of this month.' Interestingly, Colin at times considered the unthinkable: what life might be like under a German occupation. He was particularly concerned with the fate of Neville Chamberlain and speculated that 'in the event of British defeat – God forbid – he would be produced like Laval and old Pétain. I cannot understand just why Churchill does not kick him out.'

While Churchill and many Britons were doing their utmost to convince President Roosevelt of the necessity of joining with Britain to resist German aggression, 18-year-old Colin had his own thoughts about the USA. He believed that the developments in the war to date had now obliged the USA to 'realise how dependent they were upon us':

America would not help us at all by entering into this war. They are in greater danger from the Nazis than ourselves if only they but realised it. Riddled with fifth column, a bastard race, with a conflict of opinion they must maintain a two-ocean navy, which they can't.

Colin's thoughts and feelings reflect the mindset of a comparatively immature youth, but the war predictably impinged on his life in a way that he had not thought possible. On 21 August, a friend of his family, Mrs Block, called to say that her neighbor had been killed in an air raid: 'a bomb fell directly on her Anderson shelter. Her road had been machine-gunned.' Needless to say, this reawakened Colin's wishes to fight again and he drifted off into thoughts of joining the RAF:

There is nothing I would like better in this world than to be a fully-fledged fighter pilot awaiting a gigantic air offensive, lounging on the rough grass talking with Pete and Steve ... by the side of our aircraft as we awaited the signal to scramble.

While Colin's youthful bravado kept his and his friends' spirits up through this episode and many other minor raids, involving sparse formations of German aircraft, as the days passed through the summer the bombing intensified and Colin's mood darkened slightly. On 28 August he wrote: 'I cannot say how tired I am. I have never known how much sleep means. Since the early hours of Friday morning the Nazi bombers have been over continuously, in consequence we have had warning after warning.'

Colin's description of this event is particularly interesting, as it sheds light on the opinions of ordinary people on the ground towards the bombing. Colin thought that 'nuisance bombers,' as their title suggests, were more of a problem than the large-scale raids. The 'nuisance' aircraft came over singly or in pairs and their aim was simply to prompt air-raid sirens and precautions on the ground. Colin said, 'It is obvious that these raiders are sent only to shake our morale. It is these that are responsible for keeping all Londoners awake and in their shelters for hours every night.' The net result was that many people, responding directly to this German tactic, chose to demonstrate their defiance and their need for sleep, by 'taking the risk of staying in bed when they [the bombers] come over.'

Colin, true to his ideas, 'mostly stay[ed] in bed ... it was impossible during the early hours of Tuesday to do so, however, as every ten minutes or so for 6 hours the German raiders passed right over our flat.' Colin's thoughts on all of this were simple: 'I may be tired and somewhat depressed, but by God all this only makes us the more determined to smash blasted Hitler once and for all. The whole of Britain is now more determined than ever.'

This determination, which many have subsequently termed the spirit of the Blitz, was to be severely tested in the coming weeks as the German raids intensified. On Monday 9 September, Colin's tone changed considerably. Gone was the jaunty defiance and cockiness, and in its place was a genuine sense of shock:

London, my London, is wounded, bloody. The sirens sounded last night at 7.59 and straightway [sic] 'planes were diving and booming overhead. I saw a whole ring of anti-aircraft fire mark out Clapham Common high in the sky ... Becton gasworks has been hit ... we stayed in the shelter for a while, but I kept rushing around with my binoculars. At one period the firing was so intense I dare not risk the 18 yards' run to the shelter and stood against a concrete wall, flat. The 'all-clear' sounded at 5.30 am.

But worse was to come. Colin, of course, had to make his way to work that day, exhausted and strained from the excitement and lack of sleep of the previous night. After taking the underground as far as Bank, he ventured out as far as Princes Street and was greeted by a scene of utter devastation along 'a Princess Street hitherto unknown to me.'

Cars packed the road, people rushed here and there, calm and collected, fire services, ambulances. Refugees from the East End, cars and bikes, luggage and babies all poured from [the] Aldate direction ... a high explosive bomb had fallen clean in the middle of Threadneedle Street, just missing the Bank's main entrance and somehow missing the old Royal Exchange. Here in the heart of the City ... next door to my office, always considered by me as untouchable, had descended the cold and bloody stab of Hitler. In the office the windows were cracked and smashed ... dust and earth covered my chair and then I beheld the 3rd floor. No windows, debris, dirt. I was staggered as I beheld the spectacle. I took myself to the roof with my binoculars and saw the most appalling sights. All over the heart of the City fires were burning, hoses playing ... I cannot describe my feelings, they were all too dumbfounded and I was incredulous.

Colin's diary takes an abrupt turn at this juncture. He writes:

I knew then that my diary is not 'exciting' reading of happening to be envied, it does not really show the spirit of glamour which I take from these raids, but it simply shows the callousness, the futility of war. It depicts bloody people, smashed bodies, tragedy, the breaking up of homes and families. But above all, high above this appalling crime the Nazis perpetrate, there is something shining, radiating warmth above all these dead and useless bodies, it is the spirit, the will to endure, which prevails.

Colin Perry joined the merchant navy in the autumn of 1940 and on 17 November joined HMT *Strathallan* as the ship's writer. He survived the war and published his diary in 1971.

The end of the beginning

At the end of 1943, the position of Adolf Hitler's Germany looked remarkably different from that of the end of 1941. In December 1941, Hitler's empire had stretched from the Atlantic seaboard of France as far east, nearly, as Moscow. By the end of 1943 the western border remained, but in the east the limit of German expansion was moving slowly, but remorselessly, westwards.

Much had happened between 1939 and 1943. Germany's star, so long in the ascendant, was at last beginning to wane. The reasons for this are several. First, the entrance of the United States into the war in December 1941 changed the whole strategic complexion of the conflict. Hitler's presumptive decision, taken on 11 December 1941, to declare war on the USA is still a curious one. Was it a foolish and ultimately fatal decision or rather a natural response to what was something of an inevitability?

President Roosevelt's support of the British war effort to date had been considerable, and American sympathy was clearly on the side of the British and against Nazi Germany. The USA's actions, before the German declaration of war, were hardly the actions of a state intent on maintaining her neutrality. The Lend-Lease Act, whereby Britain's productive shortfall in war materials was redressed on a pay-later arrangement, dramatically altered Britain's military fortunes when she was at a particularly low ebb. However, Roosevelt still had many dissenters at home, who opposed American participation in the war in Europe. Hitler's decision removed any reason for hesitancy, as did the Japanese strike at the US Pacific Fleet at Pearl Harbor, which provided ample demonstration, if one were needed, that the USA could no longer sit on the sidelines.

Through the early months of 1943, the western allies were preparing their plans and harboring the resources necessary to launch Operation Overlord, the invasion of occupied France. At the end of 1943, Hitler's European empire was still a mighty edifice. Already, however, its borders were being rolled back in the east and in the south. The Red Army success at Stalingrad in early 1943, and in August 1943 in the enormous tank battle of Kursk, would prove significant (see *The Second World War (5) The Eastern Front* in this series).

The German attack on the Kursk salient was the last major offensive that Germany mounted in the east. The offensive, originally planned for early May 1943 – the first time that the ground was sufficiently hard to bear large-scale movement of heavy equipment after the spring thaw – was delayed considerably. Only in early July did Hitler give the order to commence the attack. Hitler's reluctance to commit his forces sooner was based on a belief that the longer he delayed, the stronger his armored formations would be. Also greater numbers of the new Panther tank could be deployed. Large quantities of new weapons were produced by Germany's now almost fully mobilized economy, but the delay also gave the Soviets additional breathing space to reorganize, reequip, and prepare their defenses in depth.

The net result may be seen as sweeping away many of the assumptions on which the Second World War was grounded. The German Wehrmacht, the instigator of fast, maneuver-style *Blitzkrieg*, was committed by its Commander-in-Chief to an attritional assault on prepared enemy positions, and in doing so played to their strengths not those of the Germans. Hitler, increasingly assuming more and more direct control over his armies in the field, was now, apparently, turning his back on the audacious thinking that had characterized much of his success between 1939 and 1943. After Kursk the German army fought a long, slow retreat that would climax in the battle for Berlin itself, the capital of the Reich that was to have lasted 1,000 years.

In July 1943 the first major Allied incursions into occupied Europe occurred when the Allies invaded Sicily. Two months later, in September, they landed on the Italian mainland and began their drive north. The German forces made the most of the difficult terrain and the narrow Italian peninsula to ensure that the Allied advance would be slow, and that German troops would not be driven out of Italy until the general surrender in 1945. However, the physical presence of Allied troops on European soil was significant and indicative of the turn of the tide.

In June 1944 came two events of enormous significance for Hitler's Reich. The first, on 6 June 1944, was the Allied assault on Normandy: Operation Overlord or D-Day as it has entered the popular lexicon. This was the opening of the second front that Stalin had long demanded to take the pressure off the Red Army. Although it had taken far longer than Stalin had hoped, and caused considerable tension with the 'Grand Alliance' as a result, the Normandy landings now obliged Hitler and his increasingly hard-pressed forces to face their strategic nightmare – a war on two fronts.

While the fighting in Italy did tie down large numbers of valuable German troops and resources, Italy was always unlikely to be a decisive theater of operations. As if to demonstrate the problems and conflicting priorities of such a war, the Soviets launched their largest offensive to date on 22 June, the third anniversary of the start of Operation Barbarossa. This new offensive, Operation Bagration, succeeded in destroying Army Group Center and was a massive blow for the Wehrmacht.

Hitler's empire shrank progressively from June 1944, as the Soviets advanced

relentlessly from the east and the British–American–Canadian–Free French forces from the west. All was effectively lost for Germany, but her resistance did not slacken. In the fighting in the east, the Germans fought bitterly for every inch of ground. The knowledge of what the Soviets would exact in revenge for German behavior in the east and, for many, a fundamental ideological struggle between communism and national socialism underpinned the ferocious struggle. In the west, too, the German resistance was stiff and the Allies gained ground only slowly. British General Bernard Montgomery's plan to end the war quickly, by seizing the vital bridges over the Rhine in Operation Market Garden, was a failure and compelled the Allies to edge forward inch by inch.

In December 1944, Hitler showed again, briefly, that there still existed an offensive capability in the German war machine, launching an attack toward the Belgian port of Antwerp, from where the Allied advance was being provisioned. This campaign in the Ardennes became known as the 'Battle of the Bulge' and demonstrated once again the tactical capability of the German army. However, Germany was fast losing the ability to sustain an offensive and the fighting in the Ardennes soon petered out with no German success.

Although the German forces kept fighting until May 1945, it was a futile battle against the odds. The Soviets gave no quarter in their struggle to defeat Nazi Germany: having experienced firsthand the commitment and brutality of Nazi racial ideology, they paid the Germans out in kind. Perhaps appropriately, the Allies decided at the Yalta Conference of early 1945 that it would be the Red Army that captured Berlin, despite the astounding progress being made by the Allies in the west. The Germans made the Soviets fight for the capital, inflicting in excess of 100,000 casualties, but the Red Flag was raised on the Reichstag, a dominant image of the Second World War.

The world at war

At the end of 1943 the world was poised on the brink of the final act of the Second World War. In 1944 the Second World War was effectively decided beyond any doubt. The three Allied powers, Britain, the USA, and the Soviet Union, would now combine effectively for the first time, bringing their resources to bear against Nazi Germany. The final victory, as well as being a triumph for the alliance against Germany, also marked, dramatically, the end of European global hegemony. It was the USA and the Soviet Union that would be the dominant forces in the world hereafter.

Between 1939 and 1943 the Second World War had grown from a comparatively localized conflagration centered, as so many wars had previously been, on western Europe, to encompass virtually the whole globe. Only the continent of the Americas escaped the ravages of war, although the localized effects of the 'Battle of the River Plate' and Japanese 'fire-balloons' on the west coast of the USA served to remind Americans of what the wider world was experiencing.

The war that had begun in Europe had spread to the Far East (see *The Second World War (1) The Pacific War* in this series). Japanese aggression swiftly deposed the colonial regimes of the British (in Malaya, Singapore, and Burma), the French (Indo-China), and the Dutch (Dutch East Indies). However, Japanese aggression had also brought the USA into the war, and the entrance of the United States tipped the balance of the war decisively in favor of the Allies. The vast economic potential of the USA, once harnessed effectively, out-produced the Axis decisively, although numbers of weapons alone are not the most significant determinant.

By early 1943 the war economy of the USA was beginning to influence the fortunes

of all the Allied forces. In January, British Prime Minister Winston Churchill and US President Franklin Roosevelt met for a major summit at Casablanca, North Africa. Following their deliberations they issued a joint ultimatum to Germany, demanding that she surrender 'unconditionally.' This was a major development; it effectively ruled out a negotiated peace in the future. Adolf Hitler and many leading Nazis continued to believe that some form of *rapprochement* was still possible with the two western allies because of the inherent tensions present in their alliance with the Soviet Union. However, despite these German hopes of a separate peace, which prompted Heinrich Himmler, the head of the SS and Gestapo, to attempt negotiations with the British and Americans in the last weeks of the war, the unlikely alliance of East and West, capitalist democracies and communist dictatorship, held firm until the defeat of Germany.

The 'unconditional surrender' ultimatum nevertheless galvanized the German populace. Whatever they may have felt about the rights and wrongs of the war, and irrespective of the common cause that the average German might or might not have felt with the Nazi Party, after the Casablanca ultimatum it was obvious that there was no way out for Germany. Unconditional surrender obliged Germany to fight on until she was defeated, totally.

The Germans also fought on for the same reasons that had prompted the outbreak initially. Put simply, a state that had been built on ideas of racial superiority was unlikely to seek to negotiate a peace, even if one had been on offer. And, as the Allies frequently pointed out, such an option did not exist. The extent to which all Germans were avid believers in all aspects of Nazi ideology has always been an area of considerable debate. Certainly, however, even those who opposed the Nazi regime had little option but to either keep quiet or face arrest and death, so strong was the security apparatus of Nazi Germany.

The brutal fashion with which Nazi Germany had waged the war also ensured that her opponents' determination to see the conflict through to a decisive conclusion was total. Nazi Germany's commitment to the ideas of racial supremacy made their dogged resistance all the more determined, as did their increasingly firm belief in ultimate victory. Arthur Harris, the man in charge of Bomber Command, once said of Hitler's Germany that 'they have sown the wind and, now, they shall reap the whirlwind.' In 1944 and 1945, Hitler's Germany was to reap the whirlwind in no uncertain fashion.

Further reading

Addison, Paul, *The Road to 1945:British Politics and the Second World War* (London 1994 [1975])

Bell, Philip, *The Origins of the Second World War* (1986).

Bond, Brian, *British Military Policy between the Two World Wars* (Oxford, 1980)

— *France and Belgium, 1939-40* (London, 1975)

Bullock, Alan,. *Hitler: A Study in Tyranny* (London, 1965)

Calvocoressi, Peter and Guy Wint, *Total War: Causes and Courses of the Second World War* (London, 1995 [1972]).

Chapman, Guy, *Why France Fell* (London 1968)

Churchill, Winston, *The Second World War*, 6 vols (London, 1948-51).

Deighton, Len, *Fighter: The True Story of the Battle of Britain* (London, 1978)

Foot, M.R.D., *SOE in France* (London, 1966)

Haestrupp, Jorgen, *European Resistance Movements 1939-45* (Westport, Conn, 1981)

Hastings, Max, *Bomber Command* (London 1979)

Horne, Alistair, *To Lose a Battle: France 1940* (London 1999 {1969])

Irving, David, *Hitler's War* (London, 1977)

Keegan, John, *The Second World War*

Kieser, Egbert, *Hitler on the Doorstep: Operation Sea Lion* (trans. Helmut Bogler, London, 11997)

Kitchen, Martin, *A World in Flames: A Short History of the Second World War in Europe and Asia 1939-45* (London, 1990).

Levine, Alan, *The Strategic Bombing of Germany* (New York, 1992)

Maier, Klaus (ed.), *Germany's Initial Conquests in Europe: Germany and the Second World War* (Oxford, 1991)

Marwick, Arthur (ed.), *Total War and Social Change* (London, 1988)

Millet, Allan R., and Williamson Murray (eds), *Military Effectiveness: The Second World War* (London, 1999).

Overy, Richard, *Why the Allies Won* (New York, 1996).

Ray, John, *The Battle of Britain: New Perspectives – Behind the Scenes of the Great Air War* (London 1999)

Taylor, A.J.P., *The Origins of the Second World War* (Oxford, 1963)

Weinberg, Gerhard, *A World at Arms: A Global History of World War 2* (Cambridge, 1994).

Index

Related titles from Osprey Publishing

AIRCRAFT OF THE ACES (ACES)
Experiences and achievements of 'ace' fighter pilots

AVIATION ELITE (AEU)
Combat histories of fighter or bomber units

COMBAT AIRCRAFT (COM)
History, technology and crews of military aircraft
Contact us for details of titles in these series – see below

To order any of these titles, or for more information on Osprey Publishing, contact:

Osprey Direct (UK) Tel: +44 (0)1933 443863 Fax: +44 (0)1933 443849 E-mail: info@ospreydirect.co.uk

Osprey Direct (USA) c/o MBI Publishing Toll-free: 1 800 826 6600 Phone: 1 715 294 3345

Fax: 1 715 294 4448 E-mail: info@ospreydirectusa.com

www.ospreypublishing.com

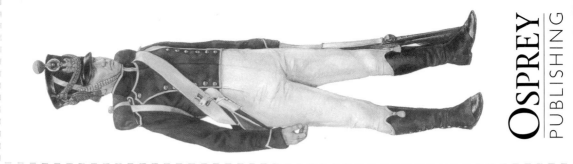

FIND OUT MORE ABOUT OSPREY

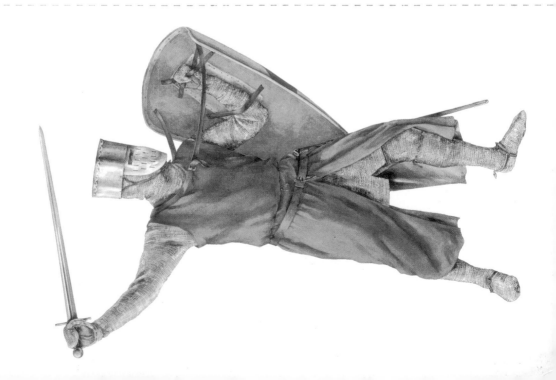

www.ospreypublishing.com

call our telephone hotline
for a free information pack

USA & Canada: 1-800-826-6600
UK, Europe and rest of world call:
+44 (0) 1933 443 863

Young Guardsman
Figure taken from *Warrior 22:
Imperial Guardsman 1799–1815*
Published by Osprey
Illustrated by Christa Hook

Knight, c.1190
Figure taken from *Warrior 1: Norman Knight 950 – 1204AD*
Published by Osprey
Illustrated by Christa Hook

POSTCARD